What Do We Believe?

by Andrew R. Rappaport

Striving
FOR
Eternity

Striving for Eternity Ministries
StrivingForEternity.org

What Do They Believe?

Striving for Eternity Press

First Edition, corrected, Soft Cover 2017

"When anyone takes Scripture in their hands and reads it, something remarkable occurs. As our eyes look over its words we are so often unaware that those words have been passed down through the centuries, through the millennia, under the providential care of the Divine. As with those originally inspired to record them, these same words come to us with a purpose. They are laden with meaning and brimming with sovereign power because they are truly the utterances of God, exhaled by Him—breathed out—for our illumination, for our salvation, and for our perpetual reconciliation with Him.

"Yet the message of the Bible—its meaning—can be challenging to comprehend. In *What Do We Believe?* Andrew Rappaport has given us a systematic theology that captures and clarifies the fundamental elements of the Christian faith—the core doctrines revealed to us in the fullness of Scripture. He has carefully, diligently, and astutely explained what the Bible means by what it says and, thus, what we believe. It is, blessedly, implicitly infused, not only with Andrew's finesse as an apologist, but also with his Gospel passion as an evangelist.

"*What Do We Believe?* is a work that, not only elucidates what is often unapproachable or avoided by many, but also serves as an invaluable discipling tool to help perpetuate the believer's responsibility to teach what accords with sound doctrine. *What Do We Believe?* is a must-have resource for the arsenal of every Christian and a robust explanation of the Christian faith for the skeptic."

—Bud Ahlheim
Christian Writer

"Andrew Rappaport has written a great systematic theology resource. This book takes the core doctrines of the Christian faith and breaks them down so that any person, with any level of theological knowledge, can grow in doctrinal understanding. The text is solidly backed by numerous biblical citations which, not only refer to the passages in which each doctrine is based, but ensure that the entire context of the passage is included in the citation. These citations give the reader clear evidence of the sound biblical nature of what is being discussed.

"Readers will find that Andrew Rappaport addresses several doctrines by looking at the various theological camps within orthodoxy. He makes an effort to be fair in his representations of those theological differences while making the case he feels to be the best biblical explanation for that doctrine. As such, some readers may find rare disagreement in the representations made; however, all of the doctrines discussed are well within orthodoxy. Thus, readers can benefit from reading and understanding the book's positions, even in areas of disagreement occur.

"This book would greatly benefit all Christians who desire to grow in their understanding of biblical theology, regardless if they be a novice or a studied theologian. I recommend that Christians take the time to read and study this text thoroughly. As we grow in our knowledge of the doctrines set forth in Scripture, we will grow in our love for God. *What Do We Believe?* will inform and nurture growth in anyone who desires to have that happen."

—Chris Hohnholz
Host of Voice of Reason Radio

Although many Christians might remain indifferent to the topic, Christian doctrine really does matter. Issues involving essential issues are crucial and must be agreed upon by believers, while the peripheral issues are those that we can agree to disagree on. Using visual charts and a readable style, Andrew Rappaport lays out a systematic theology with the goal of explaining those important issues that need to part of our everyday conversation. It behooves every Christian to pick up a book like What Do We Believe? and, with Bible in hand, see what has been said and learn from it. This is a wonderful primer for the layperson to better understand Christian theology. I highly recommend it!

--Eric Johnson

Mormonism Research Ministry

M.Div. Bethel Seminary San Diego

"*What Do We Believe?* is a wonderful book to use in Bible studies to go over the basic Christian doctrines. The thing that sets this book apart is the author's personal witnessing experience. There are certain questions and attacks that Christians who share their faith hear over and over again.

"This book is a wonderful tool to help Christians witness to others using the Bible. Andrew Rappaport gives evangelists answers to common questions so they can more effectively present the Gospel to those who need to hear it.

What Do We Believe? will be used in our ministry to train up Christians to go out and share their faith."

—Jenifer Pepling
President Christian Collegian Network
ChangeYourCampus.com

"*What Do We Believe?* is a crisp systematic theology with just a dash of apologetics. Concise and practical; made-to-order for the new believer."

—Blair Radney
Hearts for the Lost

What Do We Believe?

Table of Contents

Foreword

Phil Johnson

When I became a Christian in 1971, it seemed every believer I met was obsessed with signs of the Second Coming. The Late Great Planet Earth was at the top of the New York Times' Bestseller List. End-times speculation was everywhere in the evangelical community. Prophetic themes were standard fare in Christian music, films, conferences, and countless books. For a while after my conversion, I had the impression eschatology was the only field of doctrine that really mattered.

Then someone gave me a little book by Robert J. Little, a seasoned teacher who had recently retired as Radio Pastor of WMBI radio in Chicago. The book, titled Here's Your Answer, was a collection of Pastor Little's replies to listeners who had phoned in with questions about a large range of biblical doctrines. The question that first caught my eye and got me thinking seriously about doctrine is such a common concern that—as I now look back on those days—I'm amazed it had not yet even occurred to me: Can a born-again person lose his or her salvation? Pastor Little said no, but I wanted to know for sure.

Shortly after obtaining that book, I located a church in my community where it was obvious both pastor and people had a deep love for Christ and a high view of Scripture, so I applied to be baptized and join the church. During my baptism interview the pastor asked if I had any questions about the church, what they believed and taught, or any other biblical issues. So I put that troublesome question to him: "Now that I'm saved, is there any possibility that I might be lost again?"

He answered as briefly as possible, saying no; he believed the Bible is clear in teaching that eternal life is truly eternal. Salvation is forever. He quoted Romans 11:29: "The gifts and the calling of God are irrevocable."

"Nevertheless," he said, "that's an issue you will need to study and come to a firm conviction of your own. You need to base all your convictions on what is taught in Scripture, not on the word of any individual. The question of whether believers are eternally secure or not is one of the contested points in the classic debate between Calvinism and Arminianism. That has been a long-standing matter of controversy between two totally different Protestant doctrinal perspectives. Don't take my word for it. Study it for yourself."

So I committed myself to do that. I didn't really even grasp whether my pastor was saying he agreed with the Calvinists or not. I wasn't sure what denomination "Calvinism" was, or why they were at odds with the nation of Armenia (that's what I thought he said). But I would be leaving home for college a few weeks after that, so I put this at the top of my agenda of things to do during my first semester at college: I want to learn the differences between Calvinists and Armenians, and in the process I hope to get a better understanding of what the Bible says about the security of salvation.

My first year in college I was enrolled in a small state college in southern Oklahoma. The school library included a multi-volume encyclopedia of religion. So I borrowed that book and began to investigate the Armenian Church. While looking for the entry on "Armenian" theology, I found a lengthy article on Arminianism, and I soon realized that was what my pastor at home had been talking about.

The article summarized Arminianism in five points, and as I read them, my first impression was that I was inclined to agree with the Arminians against Calvinism on four of their five points. The only doctrine of the Calvinists I found persuasive at that time was the doctrine of the perseverance of the saints. The article included the Calvinists' biblical arguments in support of that doctrine, and by the time I was done reading it, I was convinced that no one could ever snatch me out of the hand of the Good Shepherd, much less steal me from His Father's hand (John 10:28-29).

My second impression, and the thought that has stayed with me ever since, is that biblical theology is a huge, multifaceted subject, and it is not something to be studied superficially or handled in a slapdash manner. I came away from reading that article convinced that I could not possibly master everything important in biblical doctrine even if I spent a lifetime studying. But I was eager to devote myself to the task.

Forty-six years later, I still approach the study of theology with that same attitude.

After that first year in college, I transferred to Moody Bible Institute so I could learn the Bible and its doctrines in the classroom, and not merely as extracurricular material. In one of my first classes, part of our required reading was a simple paperback titled Know What You Believe, by Paul Little. (Coincidentally, he was the son of Robert Little, the pastor whose book of answers had first prompted me to consider questions about doctrine.)

Know What You Believe was released by Inter-Varsity Press in 1970, and by 1972 it was being widely read among my generation of new believers. It was a very basic overview of essential Bible doctrines—an entry-level course in theology for many who had come to Christ in the Jesus Movement. I found it a thousand times easier to understand than the religious encyclopedia in my secular college's library, and it further opened my mind to realms of biblical and theological issues I knew were important and longed to look into. The book was by no means deep or ponderous, and I was relieved to discover that doctrine could be taught and explained in terms that a novice like me could easily grasp. Paul Little didn't delve into the debated issues between Calvinists and Arminians. But what he covered he covered well, with solid biblical proofs for the positions he took. Reading that book helped establish the foundation of core biblical truths that I have continued to build on for more than four decades.

I'm grateful that resources like that stirred a desire in me to read more, learn more, and dig deeper. (I'm now in full agreement with Calvinism against Arminian doctrines, by the way.) But I still approach Bible doctrine with the same sense that "Such knowledge is too wonderful for me; it is high; I cannot attain it" (Psalm 139:6). As a student of biblical doctrine, I pray, like David, that "my heart is not lifted up; my eyes are not raised too high; I do not occupy myself with things too great and too marvelous for me" (Psalm 131:1).

In that same spirit Andrew Rappaport has given us this wonderful volume. Andrew was gifted with an unusual knack for conveying the hard truths in easy-to-understand words. This all-new work, What Do We Believe? is a perfect resource for any beginning-level Christian, but this work has much more meat on its bones than any of the books I was given as a new Christian.

Andrew is an eager open-air evangelist and a skilled teacher. He founded Striving for Eternity Ministries, and he has trained and motivated countless others to do personal evangelism. A common deficiency among young men who do a lot of one-to-one witnessing is that they aren't always keen to move beyond the most basic gospel truths—"the elementary principles of the oracles of God . . . milk and not solid food" (Hebrews 5:12).

Andrew is of a different mind concerning truth and doctrine; he is a discipler, not merely an evangelist. He has a keen desire to know and understand the whole counsel of God, and an eager heart for encouraging others not only to "long for the pure milk of the word, so that by it you may grow in respect to salvation" (1 Peter 2:2), but also to acquire an appetite for the meat of the Word as well. And he has given us an extremely valuable tool for that very purpose.

You'll turn to this book as a treasured resource again and again. I hope you will also pass it around among those who will benefit from it. And "let us press on to maturity" (Hebrews 6:1).

Chapter 1

Authority

We believe the authority for Christianity is Scripture alone.

In fact, the statement above is so important that it sparked the reformation of Christian thought in the sixteen century. This critical Christian doctrine means that, for the Christian, the Bible is the ultimate authority for faith and practice and that the *only* authority for life and godliness is Scripture, not men (i.e., priests or leaders), church traditions, councils, or creeds. The Bible is the very Word of God written through men.

Some people claim to trust in Scripture but do not trust in it alone—they trust in the Bible plus something else. If a person puts anything above or equal in authority to God's Word, that object—not Scripture—will be the ultimate authority in his or her life. We can put our ultimate trust in man's word or God's Word, but never both.

The Bible is God's special self-revelation, limited in space and time and is directed to various, designated individuals. Peter states, *"For no prophecy was ever produced by the will of man, but men spoke from God as they were carried along by the Holy Spirit"* (2 Peter 1:21).

The accepted books and writings that make up the Bible are the 39 Old Testament books and 27 New Testament books without any of the additional writings commonly known as the Apocrypha, which were not accepted as canonized Scripture until the Council of Trent (1546 AD). The Bible provides the only inerrant (without error) and absolutely authoritative, propositional knowledge of God that exists.

The Bible alone is authoritative for faith and practice because it is God's self-revelation—the revelation of One who has the right and power to command compliance in thought and action upon His rational creatures (Acts 17:30-31; Romans 15:15). Therefore, the Bible supremely defines what we are to believe and how we are to conduct ourselves, providing us with the ultimate basis of authority for determining what is right and wrong.

Revelation

The term "revelation" refers to the divine act of communicating to man what man otherwise would not know. It is God's self-disclosure to man. There are two reasons why revelation was necessary: 1) because God is, by His nature, inaccessible to man (Isaiah 55:9) and 2) because of the fall, mankind broke their fellowship with God (Genesis 3:24). In studying the topic of revelation, there are two broad categories into which all of our understanding of revelation falls into: natural revelation and special, or supernatural, revelation. But, before we look further into the two kinds of revelation, let's look at what it actually means in regards to Scripture.

First, revelation is progressive with its greatest and most complete manifestation in the person of Jesus Christ (Hebrews 1:1-2). The revelation of God did not come to one person at one time. It was a progression of revelation to more than 40 people over a span of 1,500 years.

Second, revelation is God's supernatural act of self-communication and disclosure of Himself to humankind. Through revelation, the infinite God narrates a story about Himself to finite humans.

Third, revelation is personal, since God has taken the initiative of revealing Himself to individuals for the purpose of establishing a redemptive relationship with humankind.

Fourth, these divine truths, as recorded in the Bible, are propositional—that is, they reveal the nature of God exclusively and objectively through the medium (words) of the Bible. These propositions, in turn, generally assume the character of what we know as doctrine.[1]

Natural Revelation

Natural revelation uses natural phenomena as means of revealing God. The two instruments through which God reveals Himself to all mankind are nature and conscience. Nature clearly reveals God in a universal and timeless manner (Psalm 8:1-3; 19:1-6; Isaiah 40:12-14; Acts 14:12-17; Romans 1:19-21). The conscience convinces individuals of moral right and wrong thoughts and behaviors (Romans 2:14-15; 9:1-2; 13:5; 1 Peter 2:19; 1 Corinthians 8:7, 10, 12; 2 Corinthians 1:12; 4:2).

The purpose of natural revelation is to render man inexcusable as to the existence of God (Romans 1:20) and to prepare the way for special revelation, because natural revelation has limited ability to inform the individuals about redemption (Romans 10:13-17).

Special Revelation

Special revelation interferes with the natural course of things and is supernatural both in source and mode. Uniquely of God, special revelation is supernatural, propositional, and redemptive; and due to its supernatural nature, many religions and cults have misunderstood, misused, and twisted this form of revelation.

The Bible is the form of special revelation that God uses today to communicate to people. However, in the Bible, we can see how God has also used theophanies (physical manifestations) and Anthropomorphisms (figures of speech) to reveal himself to mankind, but we must make sure that we understand how they are used so that we avoid pitfalls.

Theophanies

A theophany is a physical manifestation of God in some way. It could be manifested in nature (Exodus 13:21-22), auditory (Exodus 19:1-3), or bodily (Genesis 16:7-14; 31:11-18; Joshua 5:13-15). Many religious leaders claim to have seen theophanies. However, there are two important characteristics of a true theophany we must keep in mind: the response of the person and the message of the person.

The response of the person

The first thing we must remember is that anyone who sees or hears a theophany responds is a manner fitting of being in the presence of the Most Holy, Supremely Divine God of the Universe. The Bible records examples of people experiencing theophanies, and the response is always one of awe and worship (Isaiah 6:5; Revelation 1:17).

We see that Isaiah became overwhelmed with his sin and the sin of his people when he states, *"And I said: 'Woe is me! For I am lost; for I am a man of unclean lips, and I dwell in the midst of a people of unclean lips; for my eyes have seen the King, the LORD of hosts!'"* (Isaiah 6:5).

The message of the person

The second characteristic is that the message of the person who sees or hears a true theophany is ALWAYS consistent with Scripture and NEVER contradicts it (2 Corinthians 13:8). The message must be compared with the Scriptures for accuracy (Acts 17:11; 1 John 4:1-3).

A person who receives a true theophany will not be concerned if someone wants to compare this message against the validity of Scripture. However, if a leader expects to be trusted explicitly without questioning, then the message is not from God, because the leader is clearly purporting themselves to be the authority, not the Scriptures.

Anthropomorphisms

Anthropomorphism is a figure of speech, not to be understood literally, used by writers of Scripture in which human, physical characteristics are attributed to God for the sake of illustrating an important point. For example, Scripture sometimes speaks of the "face" or "arm" of God, even though God is revealed to be Spirit and not limited in time and space by the constraints of a physical body.

Anthropomorphisms essentially help to make an otherwise abstract truth about God more concrete. However, God is not a physical being, He is Spirit (John 4:24). It is an error to understand anthropomorphisms as literal, assuming God to have a physical body. God the Father is not a man, nor was He ever one.

For instance, to believe, based upon anthropomorphisms, that God is a physical man ignores the descriptions of God as an animal. In parts of Scripture, God is also described as having wings like a bird or other such attribute only pertaining to an animal (Psalms 36:7; 57:1; 61:4; 63:7; 91:4). If someone teaches that God has a physical body, based on anthropomorphisms, then, to be consistent, God would also have to be considered a bird or, at the very least, some half man-half bird.

Inspiration

All Scripture is inspired by God. The word *inspiration* is from a Greek compound word that means "God" and "to breathe out," giving the meaning that the Bible is God-breathed. All Scripture is breathed or spoken from the mouth of God to mankind. The writings themselves—not the writers—were inspired.

The term "inspiration" identifies the specific, supernatural work of the Holy Spirit by which He superintended (i.e., controlled and directed) the reception (i.e., His Word given to the writers) and communication (i.e., His Word received by the readers and hearers of the writing) of the divine message to mankind, such that the original writing is verbally (every word) and plenary (completely) both inerrant (i.e., without error) and authoritative. *"All Scripture is breathed out by God and profitable for teaching, for reproof, for correction, and for training in righteousness, that the man of God may be complete, equipped for every good work"* (2 Timothy 3:16–17).

God spoke in His written Word by a process of dual authorship. The Holy Spirit so superintended the human authors that, through their individual personalities and different styles of writing, they composed and recorded God's Word to man without error in the whole or in the part.

Thus, the Scriptures are completely and totally sufficient for life and godliness. Peter wrote, *"knowing this first of all, that no prophecy of Scripture comes from someone's own interpretation. For no prophecy was ever produced by the will of man, but men spoke from God as they were carried along by the Holy Spirit"* (2 Peter 1:20–21).

By virtue that the Scriptures are inspired by God, they are part of the canon. Men only *recognized* the canonical books; they did not inspire the writings, nor did they declare them to be inspired. These writings were inspired by God, whether mankind recognized it or not.

Furthermore, when we say that the Bible is inerrant, this term includes—not only the message and content of the Bible—but the actual words, tenses, and singular or plural form of nouns used in Scripture. On several occasions, the arguments of Christ and the biblical writers rested on specific words and tenses. For example, the use of the word "gods" by the psalmist was the key to Jesus' rebuttal of the Jews' charge of blasphemy:

> Jesus answered them, "Is it not written in your Law, 'I said, you are gods'? If he called them gods to whom the word of God came—and Scripture cannot be broken—do you say of him whom the Father consecrated and sent into the world, 'You are blaspheming,' because I said, 'I am the Son of God'?" (John 10:34-35).

Another example is Paul's argument with the Galatians, which hinges on the Genesis account of "seed" rather than "seeds": *"Now the promises were made to Abraham and to his offspring. It does not say, 'And to offsprings,' referring to many, but referring to one, 'And to your offspring,' who is Christ"* (Galatians 3:16).

And when discussing our eternal life, John uses the present tense "have" instead of a future tense "will have," which makes the argument that we have already obtained it when we believe versus earning it through our own works or deeds: *"I write these things to you who believe in the name of the Son of God that you may know that you have eternal life"* (1 John 5:13).

Sufficiency

Because we know that the Word of God is inspired and inerrant, we can rest assured that it is completely and totally sufficient for the believer in every area of life for faith and practice. Scripture is all that is necessary for the completing and maturing of the Christian: *"All Scripture is given by inspiration of God, and is profitable for doctrine, for reproof, for correction, for instruction in righteousness, that the man of God may be complete, thoroughly equipped for every good work"* (2 Timothy 3:16-17).

According to 2 Peter 1:16-19, the Scriptures are a greater determiner of truth than even hearing the voice of God, and they are definitely more certain than the voice of any person. Therefore, it is Scripture alone that is our ultimate basis of authority for determining what is right and wrong.

> *For we did not follow cleverly devised myths when we made known to you the power and coming of our Lord Jesus Christ, but we were eyewitnesses of his majesty. For when he received honor and glory from God the Father, and the voice was borne to him by the Majestic Glory, "This is my beloved Son, with whom I am well pleased," we ourselves heard this very voice borne from heaven, for we were with him on the holy mountain. And we have the prophetic word more fully confirmed, to which you will do well to pay attention as to a lamp shining in a dark place,*

until the day dawns and the morning star rises in your hearts (2 Peter 1:16-19).

Moreover, absolutely no human reasoning needs to be added to Scripture, nor does anything need to be replaced to meet the needs of the believer for life and living. God commands that no part—no matter how small—should ever be added or subtracted from the Bible. See the following examples in Scripture:

Deuteronomy 4:2

> *"You shall not add to the word that I command you, nor take from it, that you may keep the commandments of the Lord your God that I command you."*

Deuteronomy 12:32

> *"Everything that I command you, you shall be careful to do. You shall not add to it or take from it."*

Proverbs 30:6

> *Do not add to His words, lest He rebuke you, and you be found a liar.*

Jeremiah 26:2

> *"Thus says the Lord: Stand in the court of the Lord's house, and speak to all the cities of Judah that come to worship in the house of the Lord all the words that I command you to speak to them; do not hold back a word."*

Revelation 22:18-19

I warn everyone who hears the words of the prophecy of this book: if anyone adds to them, God will add to him the plagues described in this book, and if anyone takes away from the words of the book of this prophecy, God will take away his share in the tree of life and in the holy city, which are described in this book.

Because the Scriptures are completely sufficient as they are without additions or subtractions, for all areas of life and godliness, the Bible constitutes the only infallible rule of faith and practice for *every* generation. See these additional references:

Matthew 5:18

For truly, I say to you, until heaven and earth pass away, not an iota, not a dot, will pass from the Law until all is accomplished.

Matthew 24:35

Heaven and earth will pass away, but my words will not pass away.

John 16:12-13

"I still have many things to say to you, but you cannot bear them now. When the Spirit of truth comes, he will guide you into all the truth, for he will not speak on his own authority, but whatever he hears he will speak, and he will declare to you the things that are to come."

John 17:17

Sanctify them in the truth; your word is truth.

1 Corinthians 2:13

And we impart this in words not taught by human wisdom but taught by the Spirit, interpreting spiritual truths to those who are spiritual.

Hebrews 4:12

For the word of God is living and active, sharper than any two-edged sword, piercing to the division of soul and of spirit, of joints and of marrow, and discerning the thoughts and intentions of the heart.

Interpretation

The Scriptures where written to be understood. One of the ministries of the Holy Spirit is to illuminate the Scriptures to the mind of the child of God. The Holy Spirit indwells every believer. Therefore, true Christians do not need a "priest" to interpret for them. Christians are all "priests" and all have the same Holy Spirit indwelling them. It is the role of each Christian to diligently study to show themselves approved unto God (2 Timothy 2:15; Acts 17:11) and the Holy Spirit, in turn, will reveal the meaning of the Scriptures (1 Corinthians 2:4).

This is the importance of the "priesthood of the believer." Martin Luther argued for the private interpretation of the Scriptures. The argument against this is that people would wrongly interpret the Scriptures.

Luther said, so let it be. It is the responsibility of the believer to study, for they are directly accountable to God.

As we have seen, the Bible constitutes the only infallible rule of faith and practice. Whereas there may be many applications of any given passage of Scripture, there is but *one* true interpretation according to God. The meaning of Scripture is to be found as one diligently and prayerfully applies the normal (some would say literal), grammatical, historical method of interpretation* under the illuminating of the Holy Spirit (John 7:17; 16:12-15; 1 Corinthians 2:7-15; 1 John 2:20).

It is the responsibility of believers to ascertain carefully the true intent and meaning of Scripture, recognizing that proper application is binding on all generations. Yet, the truth of Scripture stands in judgment of men; never do men stand in judgment of it.

---

*Normal, grammatical, historical interpretation of Scripture affirms the belief that the opening chapters of Genesis present creation in six literal days (Genesis 1:31; Exodus 31:17) and makes a distinction between Israel and the Church.

Chapter 2

Biblical Reliability

We believe that the Bible is reliable as it was passed down in its copies and literal translations.

B iblical reliability is an important topic to understand because many attack Christianity due to a lack of understanding about how the Bible came to be. Many try to claim that we cannot trust the Bible, but it is our only authority from God. The only way that we can know about God objectively and absolutely is if He reveals Himself to us in some form of universal communication. The presupposition of Christianity is that God exists, and He has spoken.

This chapter will cover a topic that even most seminary graduates never tackle, unless an unbeliever challenges them. This can often be a very technical study. However, this chapter will simplify the complex as much as possible and provide sufficient information to show that the Christian Scriptures are, not only reliable, but the most reliable document of ancient history.

Refuting the Critics

One of the most common questions non-believers ask is "How can you claim that God wrote the Bible if it was actually written by men?" It is a tricky question to answer because men did write the Bible, but God also wrote it. The reason most non-believers ask this question is because they want to claim that, if men wrote it, the Bible cannot be trusted. However, men have written everything taught to us, and they trust other things that they have learned from men; and, most importantly, what makes the Bible trustworthy is not the fact that men wrote it, but the fact that God, who cannot lie and is faithful and true, authored and inspired it. We believe and trust in an infallible Author, which is why Christians get their authority from the Word of God alone, *Sola scriptura*.

We have talked about the Bible being without error and without flaw in the original writings, but the challenge is that we do not have any original manuscripts of the Bible presently—at least, as far as anyone knows. Additionally, the many manuscripts that we have today have some variants between them.

Daniel Wallace states, "A textual variant is simply any difference from a standard text (e.g., a printed text, a particular manuscript, etc.) that involves spelling, word order, omission, addition, substitution, or a total rewrite of the text."[2] Each time that we have a variant between manuscripts, it becomes what is called a "variant reading." We can have several variant readings for the same word between many manuscripts. You could have some manuscripts that read the same Greek phrase as, "Our Lord Jesus Christ," "Jesus Christ our Lord," "the Lord Jesus," or "our Lord Christ," and these would count as four variant readings.

The more manuscripts you have, the more possible variant readings you could have. If you only have one manuscript, then you have no variants, but then you cannot tell if that one is a copy or if it is the original because you have nothing with which to compare it. Therefore, the larger the number of manuscripts we have, the better the opportunity is to discover where all these variants could be in the text.

Scholars argue that the number of variant readings is about 400,000 in the New Testament. That sounds like a large number, especially when you consider that there are only about 138,200 words in the Greek New Testament. This would mean there are three times the number of variant readings than there are words in the New Testament.

The reason for this is that scholars count each change, even of the same word between multiple manuscripts, as an individual variant. Therefore, a single word could have dozens of variants. It would be much more accurate to count only the number of words that actually changed between all the different manuscripts.

So, we needed a more precise way to define things—a base text to compare all of the other manuscripts against. Fortunately, Hodges and Farstad provided that in *The Greek New Testament according to the Majority Text* in 1985. They listed in the footnotes all the places where the majority of manuscripts disagreed with the Nestle-Aland text (a Greek manuscript). When you compare the words with a base text, the variant total comes to 6,577.[3]

But, in all actuality, the fact that there are different manuscripts or variants between manuscripts should not cause concern regarding the authority of the Scripture. As we will see, due to the large number of manuscripts, we can identify where these changes occurred, and this knowledge reveals that not a single Biblical doctrine is affected by these variants. Furthermore, with most of these changes, we can more easily determine the original meaning of the text.

If you read Bart Ehrman, he makes it sound like the Bible's original meaning is lost forever. In his book, *Misquoting Jesus*, he tries to make this point. Ehrman's greatest example of why we cannot determine the original meaning of the Bible is that some manuscripts refer to Jesus as a "carpenter" and others refer to Him as the "son of a carpenter." In this example, the meaning of the text does change, and we cannot get back to the original meaning. But, there is no biblical doctrine based on whether Jesus is a carpenter or the son of a carpenter. In fact, both could be true. If this is the best example of a "lost original meaning," then we have nothing to fear.

In his book, *Zealot: The Life and Times of Jesus of Nazareth*, Reza Aslan tries to make the same case, and yet you can throw out all his work before the first chapter begins. In the introduction, he states that he is basing his research on a document called "Q" (German: *"Quelle"* meaning "source"). Then he states, "Although we no longer have any physical copies of this document, we can infer its contents by compiling those verses that Matthew and Luke share in common but that do not appear in Mark."[4]

In other words, he has no evidence for anything he is stating. The reality is that there are no physical copies of Q and there are no references to Q in any ancient text or history. Basically, there is no evidence that Q ever existed. Scholars make up this document Q and then criticize the

Bible based on a document that has no record of ever having existed. Most people would call that a fairytale.

Category of Variants

As we talk about these variants, it would be helpful for us to define the types of variants and the problems, or rather, the lack thereof that they cause (see Figure 1). The majority of these variants—75% to be exact—are "spelling errors or punctuation." One thing to remember is that there was no punctuation and spacing between words in the manuscripts for the first 800 years of the New Testament.

Also, the adding of spaces can change the meaning of the text, depending on where you add the spacing. For example, think about the following letters: "GODISNOWHERE." You can add spaces to make two very different sentences: "God is now here" and "God is nowhere." Which is correct?

While the misspelling of words can change the meaning of a text base, we must, however, remember the value of context, which often gives us a very obvious way to determine the correct meaning. So, in most cases of these spelling errors, we can easily conclude which is the original.

The second largest category of variant, 19%, is "not meaningful but viable." Viable means that we cannot get back to the original text. This means that the variant does not change the meaning of the text in any way. Therefore, these do not represent an issue for the understanding of the meaning of the Scriptures at all.

The third largest category, 5%, is those variants that are "meaningful but not viable." Therefore, with these variants, the only way we can get back to the original text is either by the context or, more often, from the numbers of other manuscripts to which we can compare the variant.

The last type of variant is the smallest—less than 1%—but the most significant: "meaningful and viable." These are the only ones that present a problem for Biblical scholars and those who do textual criticism because 1) they do affect the meaning of the text and 2) we cannot get back to the original text.

In summary, out of all of the variants, 99% of them either do not impact the meaning of the text or can be traced back to the original meaning. Consequently, only 1% of the variants need to concern us.

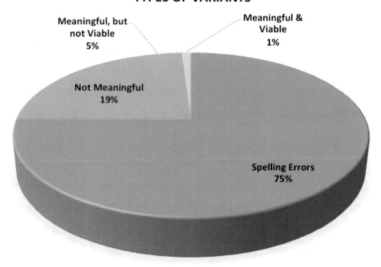

Figure 1

If we look at it in numbers, we see that 1% of the 6,577 words with textual variants in the New Testament comes to about 66 meaningful words with textual variants out of 138,162 words—a total of just 0.0476% of the New Testament. All of a sudden, when we put it into perspective, the amount of 400,000 variants with which we started does not seem so large. Therefore, we can conclude from these figures that the New Testament is 99.95% accurate.

Some will challenge this by stating that the scholars all use the 400,000 variant number. This is true because they count every variant in every manuscript. Thus, the way to compare that is to count the number of variants, which is more then 400,000, with the total number of words (roughly 138,000 in the Greek New Testament) by the total number of manuscripts (over 6500). This would be hard to calculate because many manuscripts are not complete. Many are just fragments. But the comparison would be comparing the 400,000 variants readings to over five million words in all the manuscripts, and it is still at worst a 0.08% difference. Therefore, either way we look at it, with an equal comparison, the reliability of the Bible is extremely high.

Dispelling the Myth

We must also dispel a myth that many of these liberal scholars and professing atheist bloggers tell. The Bible translation was not like the "telephone game," where one person makes one copy with a few mistakes and passes it along to another person who would make another copy but with some more mistakes and so on until the final product is nothing like the original. This is how many people depict that the Bible was disseminated and transmitted to us. However, this is not an accurate picture at all.

In the Old Testament, Jewish scribes had a process of copying that was painstaking in detail. The Jewish scribes would copy the Bible. As they copied it, they counted every single letter they had copied, and, after that, they counted every single word. With every letter, they marked a chart to keep track of the number of times that letter was used. They would do the same with the words. As a result, they could tell the frequency of every letter and every word at the end of the copy. They could then compare that to a chart that recorded all the correct number of letters and words to know if they had copied anything wrong. If it had more than three mistakes, that copy could not be used for the synagogue readings. If it had even one mistake, it could not be used for copying.

On the other hand, the process for copying the New Testament was less painstaking and more focused on efficiency. Remember, this was a time before the printing press and each one had to be copied by hand, but the first century Christians wanted to get the good news of the Gospel out to as many people as possible—and as quickly as possible. So they were not as concerned with accuracy, but were more concerned with speed and distribution.

Even though the copying of the New Testament was faster and very different than the Old Testament process, they still did not play the "telephone game," where you have only one person handling the message at a time and passing on a corrupted version of what they received.

What happened, in reality, was that someone like Paul, for instance, would write a letter of the New Testament and would have several people making copies at the same time. They would make multiple copies and give it to others to make multiple copies. These copies were spread throughout the region so that they could be duplicated and circulated farther.

Subsequently, when there were changes from copy to copy, each copy could be traced to its geographical location so that it could be seen how this change was fostered. The main difference between this process and the "telephone game" is that these copies are written down and not auditory. For that reason, each one can be checked and verified against original or older manuscripts.

Matt Slick provides a great illustration of this process on his website CARM.org,[5] showing how we can determine what was changed and where a change occurred (see Figure 2). When a word would go missing from a copy, it could be compared with the others copied in that geographical area. We then would be able to see that somewhere in that location there was a missing word in the manuscripts, but not elsewhere around the world. As we gather thousands of manuscripts from around the world, we can compare these local changes to others and discover the change.

These groups of local manuscripts became known as "manuscript families."

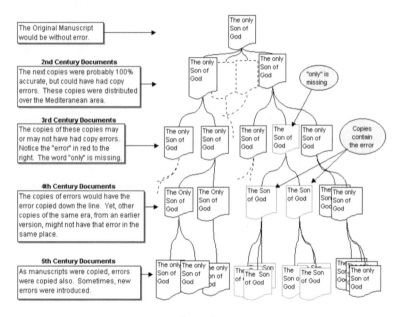

Figure 2

Factors for reliability

There are three factors that weigh heavy in the science of textual criticism:

1. Closeness of the copy to the original writing

2. Number of manuscripts

3. Geographical location

We have just seen how the number of copies and the geographical location of those copies play a role in determining the original text, but the age of the copy is also important. Remember that changes occur over time: the less time that you have, the fewer changes you should have. In other words, the closer a copy is to the original, the less likely it is that it contains changes. Using the age of the manuscript allows us to assume that there would be fewer changes.

Also, there are times when we can rely on the early church fathers for help. In some early manuscripts, the number of man mentioned in the book of Revelation was 616, instead of 666. Now, that figure does not affect any doctrine (unless you are looking at Christian end-times movies or the *Left Behind* book series). However, we have a second-century church father, Irenaeus, which spoke of this early textual variant, and he said the better manuscripts seemed to point to 666. So, the early church fathers help us to identify the corrections to some early variants.

We are consistently discovering more and more Greek manuscripts, and the numbers are adding up with many of them being very close to the original writing. With modern technology, we can now read fragments of manuscripts from papyrus that was washed and reused. This was a common practice because the materials used to write on were very expensive. Therefore, the oldest manuscripts often were reused—as good environmentalists would do—but, in this case, they were more like capitalists who wanted to save some money.

Another location for the more ancient manuscript fragments is mummies' tombs. Older Greek manuscripts would be used as scrap paper to mummify people. If people wanted to edit the text of Scripture, the trash is a place that would not be affected, and it is a good place to look.

Discovered in 1934, one of the oldest fragments we have is from the book of John dated AD 125 (called "P52"). This puts the fragment within 30+ years of the original writing, making it extremely close to the original as we will see when compared to other ancient manuscripts. Additionally, some more recent discoveries have given us fragments within the first century, only a few generations from the original writings. As of December 2014, we have over 5,824 catalogued Greek manuscripts, the average of which is about 200 pages. In total, that gives us over 1.2 million pages of Greek manuscripts. We even have over 125 Greek manuscript witnesses within the first 300 years after its writing.

As many uneducated critics argue that the Bible was edited in the fourth century, these manuscripts become important to prove these critics incorrect. Also, many Muslims argue that the Bible was corrupted after the time of Jesus. However, the Quran stated that the Bible can be trusted (Q 5:44-48), and that it was first taught during the life of Muhammad (610-632 AD). If this corruption actually occurred, we would be able to know that from these much earlier manuscripts.

In addition, as scholar Daniel B. Wallace points out: "It is not just the Greek [manuscripts] that count, either. Early on, the [New Testament] was translated into a variety of languages—Latin, Coptic, Syriac, Georgian, Gothic, Ethiopic, Armenian. These translations of the New Testament can help to get back to the original meaning of the text sometimes. There are more than 10,000 Latin [manuscripts] alone."[6]

When we examine all of the manuscripts, the best guess is that we have over 20,000 manuscripts of the New Testament. However, if we did not use any of these manuscripts, we could recreate the whole of the New Testament, except for 11 verses, from the quotations of the early church fathers alone during AD 150-200. There are over 1 million quotations from the early church fathers. When we add all the manuscripts, fragments, and quotations from the New Testament, it approaches almost 70,000 copies. Suddenly, we have a very large number of New Testament references. With all this information, it should be clear at this point that the common argument that the Bible was later edited and disseminated around the world in AD 300-500 is false.

Since we are confident in other ancient documents to tell us things like the history of Julius Caesar or the wars of the Greeks, let's see how the New Testament compares to some of these other ancient and yet trusted documents. When we examine the New Testament against the works of Homer, Demosthenes, Herodotus, Plato, Tacitus, Caesar and Pliny (see Figure 3), it is obvious that the New Testament is far more reliable than any of its closest neighbors of ancient documents, whether it is by the number of manuscripts or the time gap between the original writing and the nearest manuscript in time.

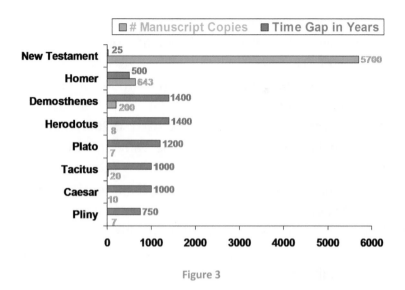

Figure 3

Mark Barry has a great visualization that brings much of this discussion together in one picture. It helps to see how the New Testament overshadows all of the other ancient documents (see Figure 4). In this illustration, he uses the size of the yellow dot to represent the number of manuscripts and the closeness to the center, and the black dot to represent the closeness of the writing to its earliest existing copies.

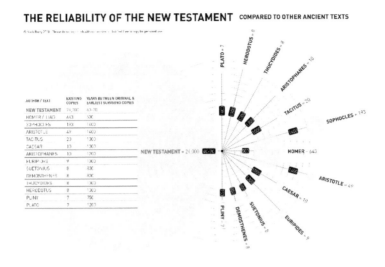

Figure 4

With all this information, we can rest on the fact that very little of the New Testament is in question, and even less of the Old Testament is. Due to the very large number of manuscripts, it helps us identify every possible variant location in the Bible, and, because of that, we know that *not one of them* affects any major Christian doctrine.

Knowing that we can trust in the reliability of the Bible is different than understanding its meaning, which is the study of hermeneutics and beyond the study of this book. However, a good resource for learning the principles of hermeneutics and to rightly interpret God's Word, can be found in the 20-lesson class on the Striving for Eternity Academy website:

StrivingForEternity.org/academy

Chapter 3

God

We believe in the One Living and True God who is three separate and distinct Persons yet one Being.

There is one living and true God (Deuteronomy 6:4; Isaiah 45:5-7; 1 Corinthians 8:4), an infinite, all knowing Spirit (John 4:24), perfect in all His attributes, one in essence, eternally existing in three Persons: Father, Son, and Holy Spirit (Matthew 28:19; 2 Corinthians 13:14), each equally deserving worship and obedience.

God's Attributes

As we see from Scripture, God orders and disposes all things according to His own purpose and grace (Psalm 145:8-9; 1 Corinthians 8:6). He is the Creator of all things (Genesis 1:1-31; Ephesians 3:9). As the only absolute and omnipotent Ruler in the universe, He is sovereign in creation, providence, and redemption (Psalm 103:19; Romans 11:36).

God also has an all-inclusive plan that He designed for His own glory, guiding all things that come to pass (Ephesians 1:11). He continually upholds, directs, and governs all creatures and events (1 Chronicles 29:11).

In God's sovereignty, He is neither author nor approver of sin (Habakkuk 1:13; John 8:38-47), nor does He abridge the accountability of moral, intelligent creatures (1 Peter

1:17). He has graciously chosen from eternity those whom He would have as His own (Ephesians 1:4-6); He saves from sin all who come to Him through Jesus Christ; He adopts all those who come to Him as his own (John 1:12; Romans 8:15; Galatians 4:5; Hebrews 12:5-9).

God is Not a Man

The essence of God is totally and completely Spirit. This is the invisible source of personality (John 1:18; Romans 1:20; Colossians 1:15; 1 Timothy 1:17; 6:15-16). God is not physical or material. Thus, God is not dependent, limited, restricted, or subject to matter or space in any way. God's Spirit is immense and omnipresent. As applied to God, God is infinite in matter.

Statements in Scripture that refer to God in physical forms are called "anthropomorphic expressions." They are figures of speech, which assist people to better understand God and/or His acts; they do not ascribe bodily parts. When Scripture states that God appeared to men in times past as a physical being, these statements are called "Theophanies." Theophanies were divine manifestations (i.e., adjustments made for man's comprehension), not glimpses of God. (See Chapter 1 for more on Theophanies.)

Trinity

The terms Trinity, Triunity or Trinitarian are not found in Scripture, but are terms we use to describe the teaching that God is one in essence or being, yet existing in three separate and distinct personalities. The Trinity refers to the doctrine of the three Persons in one God. Some falsely define this doctrine as three Persons in one Person or as three Gods in one God. Both are incorrect. These untruthful definitions are used by false teachers to make it easy to improperly refute this doctrine (i.e., a "straw man argument"). Properly defined, the Trinity is: three separate and distinct Persons in one completely and totally unified Godhead.

The concept of the Trinity is incomprehensible to man. All the attributes of God are fully true of each of the Persons or Essences of the Godhead. The doctrine of the Trinity is further proven in the doctrines of the Deity of Christ and the Deity of the Holy Spirit. *For there are three that bear witness in heaven: the Father, the Word, and the Holy Spirit; and these three are one* (1 John 5:7 NKJV).

Although this is the clearest Scripture we have on the subject of the Trinity, it does not make a strong argument against knowledgeable cult members or other opponents of this doctrine. Why? Because they may point out that this passage has a textual variant and is not even found in any of the earliest manuscripts. It only appears in eight Greek manuscripts, which seem to be translations from the Latin.

While these things are true, we should also consider how this passage appeared and remained in the text. Likely, it was something put in the sidelines by someone copying the Scriptures, and it eventually found its way into the main text. Four of the eight Greek manuscripts have this addition in the margin. However, what is important to note is that the truth of the doctrine itself was not disputed at the time when it found its way into the main text; only its placement in this text is disputed.

In addition, the following passage clearly teaches the doctrine and there are many other places in the Scripture where we see the doctrine of the Trinity. As we will see shortly, this verse is not needed to prove the Trinity of God.

Hints of the Trinity in the Old Testament

Clearly, the Old Testament places great emphasis on the uniqueness and unity of God. This foundation in understanding God was necessary in order to refute the primary religious deviation at the time, polytheism. However, even though the Old Testament emphasizes the unity of God, we still find hints to the existence of the Trinity.

The Use of Elohim

Genesis 1:1 states: *"In the beginning God* [Elohim] *created the heavens and the earth." Elohim*, a plural noun, is used with singular verbs as it is employed to describe the One, True God. Thus, we see that this name teaches the unity of God and allows for the teaching of the Trinity of God at the same time.

Some liberal theologians and Jews will state that *Elohim* was used for literary purposes and not as proof of the Trinity. But, as we have seen, specific words and letters throughout Scripture are purposeful and, in the originals, they were without error. For that reason, we can conclude that the use of a plural word with singular verbs is not literary but definitive.

The Use of Plural Pronouns

God also used plural pronouns to refer to Himself. These intimations support the plurality of the Godhead. See the following examples:

Then God said, "Let us make man in our image, after our likeness. And let them have dominion over the fish of the sea and over the birds of the heavens and over the livestock and over all the earth and over every creeping thing that creeps on the earth" (Genesis 1:26).

Then the Lord God said, "Behold, the man has become like one of us in knowing good and evil. Now, lest he reach out his hand and take also of the tree of life and eat, and live forever—" (Genesis 3:22).

And I heard the voice of the Lord saying, "Whom shall I send, and who will go for us?" Then I said, "Here I am! Send me" (Isaiah 6:8).

As mentioned above in regards to the use of *Elohim*, some argue that this plural noun use is just a literary device, but, once again, we have seen that each word of the Bible is purposeful. Others, mostly Jews, state that the plural pronouns refer to God talking with the angels. However, the context of these verses does not support that position, for we are not made in the image of angels, but in the image of God alone.

The Use of One

Many who oppose the doctrine of the Trinity claim that it contradicts the clear teaching of the Bible that there is but one God. The Hebrew word *echad* used in Deuteronomy 6:4, *"Hear, O Israel: The Lord our God, the Lord is one [echad],"* which is translated as "one," does not always refer to "oneness" in the sense of "single," but can mean "oneness" in the sense "unity." We see often that *echad* is used to refer to "one people" as a unified group of many (Genesis 11:6; 34:16,22).

The word *echad* used as "one" (meaning single) refers to God as one single Being. Note that we believe that there is only one God. This usage does not deny the Biblical view and still allows for the unity within the Godhead. The only groups that see a problem with this argument are those that try to argue that the Trinity is three gods.

Angel of the Lord

The "Angel of the Lord" in the Old Testament and other Christophanies (i.e., Theophanies that are specifically non-physical manifestations of Christ) are able to exist in one place and time, accepting worship yet still being in the heavens. In the variety of passages prophesying the coming Messiah, He is spoken of as being the same in essence as God, yet a distinct personality.

Teaching About the Trinity in the New Testament

While the Old Testament emphasized the unity of God and, at the time, allowed for the teaching of the Trinity, the New Testament clearly presents the Godhead as one in essence, yet existing in three persons.

Three Persons are Recognized as God

The Father is recognized as God

Few people argue that the Father is not recognized as God. Most people accept that the Father is God, but some think that the Father is the only Person of the Godhead. Clearly, Jesus recognized that the Father is God in John 16:27, *"for the Father himself loves you, because you have loved me and have believed that I came from God."* But what about the other two Persons of the Trinity?

The Son is recognized as God

Forty-eight percent of the four gospels refer to Jesus as God directly or indirectly, with the Gospel of John having the most at almost 67%—with many being very clear, explicit examples.

In the very first verse of his gospel, John states, *"In the beginning was the Word, and the Word was with God, and the Word was God"* (John 1:1). The reference to "the Word" is a reference to Christ as made clear in verse 14: *"And the Word became flesh and dwelt among us, and we have seen his glory, glory as of the only Son from the Father, full of grace and truth"* (John 1:14). Jesus is the Word made flesh.

In addition, the disciples of Jesus recognized Him as God. The clearest example is Jesus' encounter with Thomas after the resurrection, when he declared that Jesus was both his Lord and his God.

Eight days later, his disciples were inside again, and Thomas was with them. Although the doors were locked, Jesus came and stood among them and said,

"Peace be with you." Then he said to Thomas, "Put your finger here, and see my hands; and put out your hand, and place it in my side. Do not disbelieve, but believe." Thomas answered him, "My Lord and my God!" Jesus said to him, "Have you believed because you have seen me? Blessed are those who have not seen and yet have believed." (John 20:26–29)

We see throughout the gospels that Jesus declares that He and the Father are one, and even the enemies of Jesus, the Jewish leaders, recognized that Jesus was claiming to be God. In John chapter 10, the reaction of the Jewish leaders makes it clear that they understand Him to be making this claim:

"I and the Father are one." The Jews picked up stones again to stone him. Jesus answered them, "I have shown you many good works from the Father; for which of them are you going to stone me?" The Jews answered him, "It is not for a good work that we are going to stone you but for blasphemy, because you, being a man, make yourself God" (John 10:30–33).

The Spirit is recognized as God

In the account of Ananias and Sapphira, Peter explains that lying to the Holy Spirit is the same thing as lying to God.

But Peter said, "Ananias, why has Satan filled your heart to lie to the Holy Spirit and to keep back for yourself part of the proceeds of the land? While it remained unsold, did it not remain your own? And after it was sold, was it not at your disposal? Why is it that you have contrived this deed in your heart? You have not lied to man but to God" (Acts 5:3–4).

In his letter to Titus, Paul explains that God our Savior is the Holy Spirit. Note how Paul refers to God and the Holy Spirit interchangeably:

But when the goodness and loving kindness of God our Savior appeared, he saved us, not because of works done by us in righteousness, but according to his own mercy, by the washing of regeneration and renewal of the Holy Spirit, whom he poured out on us richly through Jesus Christ our Savior, so that being justified by his grace we might become heirs according to the hope of eternal life (Titus 3:4–7).

Three are One in Essence

We will see shortly that each Person of the Trinity shares in the attributes of God, and it is these shared attributes that display the Three are one in essence and in nature. The most obvious indication of these shared attributes is how the three Persons are used interchangeably throughout Scripture.

The Father is One with the Son

As we discussed earlier, the Gospel of John uses references to God and Jesus interchangeably. The clearest example is the first verse of John: *"In the beginning was the Word, and the Word was with God, and the Word was God"* (John 1:1).

And as we also saw in John 10:30-33, Jesus also visibly states that He and God the Father are one in essence and that this statement of Jesus was so unmistakably understood by his hearers that they wanted to stone him to death for calling Himself God.

In a similar manner, Jesus explained to Thomas that if you know Jesus then that means you know the Father— further evidence to the two being one in essence. Notice how Jesus shows the interoperability between the Father and the Son in this passage:

> "And if I go and prepare a place for you, I will come again and will take you to myself, that where I am you may be also. And you know the way to where I am going." Thomas said to him, "Lord, we do not know where you are going. How can we know the way?" Jesus said to him, "I am the way, and the truth, and the life. No one comes to the Father except through me. If you had known me, you would have known my Father also. From now on you do know him and have seen him." Philip said to him, "Lord, show us the Father, and it is enough for us." Jesus said to him, "Have I been with you so long, and you still do not know me, Philip? Whoever has seen me has seen the Father. How can you say, 'Show us the Father'? [...] Jesus answered him, "If anyone loves me, he will keep my word, and my Father will love him, and we will come to him and make our home with him (John 14:3–9, 23).

The Spirit is One with the Son

Not only are the Father and the Son one in essence— that is they share the attributes and nature of God—but the Holy Spirit and Jesus the Son are one. As with God the

Father and Jesus the Son, many passages refer to the Holy Spirit and Jesus interchangeably, indicating that they are one. If you have the Spirit, that means you have the Son; and the Spirit is truth and the Son is truth.

> *Those who are in the flesh cannot please God. You, however, are not in the flesh but in the Spirit, if in fact the Spirit of God dwells in you. Anyone who does not have the Spirit of Christ does not belong to him. But if Christ is in you, although the body is dead because of sin, the Spirit is life because of righteousness. If the Spirit of him who raised Jesus from the dead dwells in you, he who raised Christ Jesus from the dead will also give life to your mortal bodies through his Spirit who dwells in you* (Romans 8:8–11).

> *When the Spirit of truth comes, he will guide you into all the truth, for he will not speak on his own authority, but whatever he hears he will speak, and he will declare to you the things that are to come. He will glorify me, for he will take what is mine and declare it to you. All that the Father has is mine; therefore I said that he will take what is mine and declare it to you* (John 16:13–15).

The Spirit is One with the Father

Through these examples, we have seen that God the Father and God the Son are one. We also have seen that God the Son and God the Spirit are one. Lastly, we must notice that these Scriptures also explain that God the Spirit and God the Father are one.

For example, the Scriptures state that lying to the Holy Spirit is lying to God and also that, if the Holy Spirit dwells in you, then God dwells in you. Again the language in these passages makes it clear that the Scripture sees no difference between the Holy Spirit and God the Father. Read these passages again in reference to God the Father and the Holy Spirit being one:

> But Peter said, "Ananias, why has Satan filled your heart to lie to the Holy Spirit and to keep back for yourself part of the proceeds of the land? While it remained unsold, did it not remain your own? And after it was sold, was it not at your disposal? Why is it that you have contrived this deed in your heart? You have not lied to man but to God" (Acts 5:3–4).

> Those who are in the flesh cannot please God. You, however, are not in the flesh but in the Spirit, if in fact the Spirit of God dwells in you. Anyone who does not have the Spirit of Christ does not belong to him. But if Christ is in you, although the body is dead because of sin, the Spirit is life because of righteousness. If the Spirit of him who raised Jesus from the dead dwells in you, he who raised Christ Jesus from the dead will also give life to your mortal bodies through his Spirit who dwells in you (Romans 8:8–11).

Three are Distinct from Each Other

There is a unity in the Trinity yet the plurality of the Godhead is distinct from each other (Genesis 1:1-2; Psalm 110:1; Isaiah 63:7,10; Hosea 1:7; John 14:16-17, 28; Galatians 4:4). Distinction in existence does not mean there is distinction in essence. These three persons of the Godhead who are all considered divine are to be recognized as one in essence, equally existing in three personalities.

Father is distinct from the Son

Jesus clearly displayed that He is distinct from the Father. While He was on earth, Jesus claimed that He would be going to the Father, making a clear distinction between the two. He argues that there is a separation between the Father and the Son: *"You heard me say to you, 'I am going away, and I will come to you.' If you loved me, you would have rejoiced, because I am going to the Father, for the Father is greater than I"* (John 14:28).

We also see that Paul saw a distinction between God the Father and God the Son. He argues that Jesus is the form of God and did not consider it wrong to do so:

> *Have this mind among yourselves, which is yours in Christ Jesus, who, though he was in the form of God, did not count equality with God a thing to be grasped, but emptied himself, by taking the form of a servant, being born in the likeness of men. And being found in human form, he humbled himself by becoming obedient to the point of death, even death on a cross* (Philippians 2:5–8).

He also made the case that God the Father sent the Son to be born of a woman:

> *But when the fullness of time had come, God sent forth his Son, born of woman, born under the law* (Galatians 4:4).

Spirit is distinct from Father and Son

Before Jesus left the earth He told His disciples that He speaks to the Father, showing a distinction between the Son and the Father. Jesus also stated that the Father will send the Spirit after He departs. Thus, the Spirit is not only distinct from the Son but also from the Father.

> *And I will ask the Father, and he will give you another Helper, to be with you forever, even the Spirit of truth, whom the world cannot receive, because it neither sees him nor knows him. You know him, for he dwells with you and will be in you* (John 14:16–17).

Each have the Attributes of God

Attributes are distinguishing characteristics or qualities that describe a nature, being, or essence. In relation to God, attributes are those distinguishing characteristics or qualities of divine nature, which are inseparable from the idea of God and constitute what He is. We are compelled to attribute these characteristics to God. Thus, the attributes of God are permanent and inseparable qualities.

These attributes were not caused by nor affected by the works of God (i.e., creation) in any way other than that they manifest these attributes to His creation. God cannot grow or change any of His attributes. The attributes we will discuss are those that God has revealed to us. These attributes, however, are not the sum total of God. They are attributes related to God's Deity and those which God alone possesses. These attributes are only true of God, and each person of the Trinity possesses all attributes of God.

The Son Possess the Attributes of God

We see from the Scriptures that Jesus Christ possesses the attributes of God. Over and over again in the gospels, Jesus displayed these characteristics:

- Jesus is omniscient: *"But Jesus on his part did not entrust himself to them, because he knew all people and needed no one to bear witness about man, for he himself knew what was in man"* (John 2:24–25).
- Jesus is omnipresent. He states that He will be with every believer at the same time, being at all places everywhere (Matthew 28:20; Hebrews 4:13).
- Jesus is eternal: *"In the beginning was the Word, and the Word was with God, and the Word was God"* (John 1:1).
- He states that He is the "I Am," the Self-Existent: *Jesus said to them, "Truly, truly, I say to you, before Abraham was, I am"* (John 8:58).
- And He is the Alpha and Omega, the First and the Last: *"I am the Alpha and the Omega," says the Lord God, "who is and who was and who is to come, the Almighty"* (Revelation 1:8).

The Spirit Possess the Attributes of God

Just as we have seen with the Son, the attributes of God are explicitly attributed also to the Holy Spirit:

- The Holy Spirit is omnipresent as we see that there is nowhere to hide from Him: *Where shall I go from your Spirit? Or where shall I flee from your presence?* (Psalm 139:7).

- The Holy Spirit is omniscient. The Spirit searches all things and knows the things of God:

  these things God has revealed to us through the Spirit. For the Spirit searches everything, even the depths of God. For who knows a person's thoughts except the spirit of that person, which is in him? So also no one comprehends the thoughts of God except the Spirit of God (1 Corinthians 2:10–11).

Just like the Father and the Son are eternal, so is the Spirit. The Holy Spirit is called the "eternal Spirit." To be eternal means to be without beginning or ending. Self-existence is essential to being God:

how much more will the blood of Christ, who through the eternal Spirit offered himself without blemish to God, purify our conscience from dead works to serve the living God (Hebrews 9:14).

Each do the Work of God

There are primary works of God that involved all three persons of the Trinity: accepting of worship, creation, preservation, providence, the Incarnation of Jesus Christ, and the resurrection of Jesus Christ. Each person of the Trinity works independently from each other to accomplish a unified plan. The individual works are explained in some detail as the ministry of Christ and the ministry of the Holy Spirit.

Accept Worship

Each Person of the Trinity is an object of worship. God made it clear from the beginning that God and God alone should be worshipped, as He states in Exodus 20:3, *"You shall have no other gods before Me."* Yet we see many people who worshipped Jesus and saw no inconsistency:

> *And those in the boat worshiped him, saying, "Truly you are the Son of God"* (Matthew 14:33).

> *While he blessed them, he parted from them and was carried up into heaven. And they worshiped him and returned to Jerusalem with great joy* (Luke 24:51–52).

> *Therefore God has highly exalted him and bestowed on him the name that is above every name, so that at the name of Jesus every knee should bow, in heaven and on earth and under the earth, and every tongue confess that Jesus Christ is Lord, to the glory of God the Father* (Philippians 2:9–11).

Not only is God the Father and God the Son accepting of worship, but Jesus declares that the Holy Spirit is also accepting of worship. In fact, Jesus demands that we worship the Spirit in John 4:24: *"God is spirit, and those who worship him must worship in spirit and truth."*

Creation

Creation is the "the work of God in bringing all things into existence"[7] or, in more detail, "the work of God in bringing into existence the universe, including both the material and the spiritual worlds; in a more restricted sense, the bringing into existence and into its present condition the earth and the system to which it belongs."[8]

This "bringing into existence" occurred without the use of any preexisting materials. God created all that is out of nothing—without influence from anything outside of Himself and with the appearance of age. This means that things were created fully formed (i.e. trees as trees and not seeds; chickens as chickens and not eggs). God also created entirely alone, without help from anyone else:

> *Thus says the Lord, your Redeemer, who formed you from the womb: "I am the Lord, who made all things, who* alone *stretched out the heavens, who spread out the earth* by myself" (Isaiah 44:24) (Emphasis added).

This verse eliminates any idea that the Jehovah Witnesses and others have that God created Jesus and then created everything through Jesus. It is clear from Scripture that all three persons of the Trinity were involved in creation: God the Father in Genesis 1:1, God the Son in Colossians 1:16, and God the Spirit in Genesis 1:2. Furthermore, any essence involved in creation must be God, for He existed prior to the time/space continuum; thus He is eternal.

Preservation

The preserving work of God refers to His continuously maintaining and sustaining the existence of all He has created. And God is still active in the preserving work of His creation. Just as the Father is active in preservation (Nehemiah 9:6; Psalm 36:6), so is the Son (Colossians 1:17;

1 Timothy 6:13; Hebrews 1:3). In the time of Noah, God promised His continuous work of preservation (Genesis 8:21-22), and God established and uses natural laws to sustain His creation (Job 5:10; Psalm 104; Matthew 5:45; Acts 14:17).

Providence

Providence refers to God's guiding and directing work of His creation. He is actively involved in all events of His creation. In Genesis, we see how Joseph explains that God the Father was working all through his life, even when His brothers sold him into slavery. God was providentially working to protect the children of Abraham:

> When Joseph's brothers saw that their father was dead, they said, "It may be that Joseph will hate us and pay us back for all the evil that we did to him." So they sent a message to Joseph, saying, "Your father gave this command before he died: 'Say to Joseph, "Please forgive the transgression of your brothers and their sin, because they did evil to you."'" And now, please forgive the transgression of the servants of the God of your father." Joseph wept when they spoke to him. His brothers also came and fell down before him and said, "Behold, we are your servants." But Joseph said to them, "Do not fear, for am I in the place of God? As for you, you meant evil against me, but God meant it for good, to bring it about that many people should be kept alive, as they are today" (Genesis 50:15–20).

Jesus also claims that He, like the Father, is active in providence. When Jesus made this clear claim of providence, the Jews, at the time, understood that Jesus was identifying Himself as God by that claim. See the reaction of the Jews when Jesus makes this statement:

> *But Jesus answered them, "My Father is working until now, and I am working." This was why the Jews were seeking all the more to kill him, because not only was he breaking the Sabbath, but he was even calling God his own Father, making himself equal with God* (John 5:17–18).

Incarnation of Jesus Christ

The Incarnation of Jesus Christ refers to the pre-existent, second Person of the Trinity coming into time and space in a human body. Understanding the doctrine of the Incarnation is essential for people who accept Jesus' Deity but question His humanity (1 John 4:2; 2 John 4). As the early Christian confession, quoted by Paul, states:

> *"And without controversy great is the mystery of godliness:* God was manifested in the flesh, *Justified in the Spirit, Seen by angels, Preached among the Gentiles, Believed on in the world, Received up in glory"* (1 Timothy 3:16 NKJV) (Emphasis added).

It is also important to note that Jesus' coming was voluntary (Philippians 2:7), and His coming was to fulfill the Father's will. Scripture declares that the conception of Jesus was by the Holy Spirit:

> *But as he considered these things, behold, an angel of the Lord appeared to him in a dream, saying, "Joseph, son of David, do not fear to take Mary as*

your wife, for that which is conceived in her is from the Holy Spirit" (Matthew 1:20).

And the angel answered her, "The Holy Spirit will come upon you, and the power of the Most High will overshadow you; therefore the child to be born will be called holy—the Son of God" (Luke 1:35).

Resurrection of Jesus Christ

The Trinity's total participation in the resurrection of Jesus Christ displays the active role of each person of the Trinity in the plan of salvation (Acts 2:22; Galatians 1:1; John 2:19-22; Romans 8:11). The resurrection of Jesus Christ was necessary to prove the Deity of Christ.

First, we see that the Father raised Jesus from the dead:

[...] Paul, an apostle—not from men nor through man, but through Jesus Christ and God the Father, who raised him from the dead (Galatians 1:1).

Second, we see that the Son raised Himself from the dead:

Jesus answered them, "Destroy this temple, and in three days I will raise it up." The Jews then said, "It has taken forty-six years to build this temple, and will you raise it up in three days?" But he was speaking about the temple of his body. When therefore he was raised from the dead, his disciples remembered that he had said this, and they believed the Scripture and the word that Jesus had spoken (John 2:19–22).

Third, we see that the Spirit raised Jesus from the dead:

If the Spirit of him who raised Jesus from the dead dwells in you, he who raised Christ Jesus from the dead will also give life to your mortal bodies through his Spirit who dwells in you (Romans 8:11).

Conclusion

Many who deny the Trinity do so because they cannot explain it from a human perspective. Yet there are many things about God that are completely beyond our comprehension (i.e., hearing and answering all prayer; being everywhere at the same time; knowing all things; past, present, future, real, and possible in one present reality; being outside of time, etc.). No human can explain these things. We believe them because the Bible teaches these truths. The Bible teaches the reality of the Trinity of God; therefore, we believe it, whether we can explain it or not!

The Trinity is a solution to a problem, not a problem. The problem lies within whether we believe Scripture or not. For the Scripture reveals that the Father is referred to as God, the Son is referred as God, and the Spirit is referred to as God; and the Scripture teaches that each are separate and distinct Persons, and yet the same in divine essences, divine attributes, and divine works. So, if someone does not accept the teaching explained by the doctrine of God's Trinity, then they have a problem with Scripture that needs to be solved.

Chapter 4

Jesus Christ

We believe that Jesus Christ is the Almighty God, fully God and fully man; the prophesied Messiah of the Old Testament.

Although it has been difficult for men to understand throughout the ages, the Scriptures teach that Jesus Christ is fully God and fully Man: two natures in indivisible oneness. It is usually one of the two natures of Christ that are attacked or misunderstood. It is important to realize that Jesus Christ has two natures, one fully man and one fully God. Part of the reason for the confusion is that Jesus at times speaks from the limitations of His humanity even though He is God (Matthew 4:2; Luke 22:43; John 4:6; 19:28).

In the first century, Christ's Deity was not questioned but His humanity was. This causes some confusion now, because people may not realize that the New Testament writers had to defend the humanity of Christ more than the Deity of Christ. Today, it is mostly His Deity that is questioned and not His humanity. It is important to see that the Scriptures clearly teach that Jesus Christ is both God and man: the God-man.

The Deity of Christ

We see the struggle on the issue of Christ's Deity emerge after the "Christianization" of the Roman Empire. Since that time, cults have arisen that have questioned the

Deity of Jesus Christ, even though the Scriptures explicitly prove His Deity by the names, works, and attributes of Christ.

When Constantine was emperor he declared Rome a "Christian" nation. However, Christians are not Christian by birth or name, nor are they decreed. It is only through a true belief in Jesus Christ that a person becomes a Christian. During that time, many people—who were Christians in name only—found it favorable and politically expedient to talk like Christians, even though they did not believe in Jesus Christ, nor in the Holy Scriptures.

This caused a new problem since these "Christian" leaders began to debate Christian doctrine in order to argue for a belief system that they, as unbelievers, could tolerate and accept. In this regard, a conflict between true Christians and the unsaved "Christian" leaders ensued for many years. The debate went back and forth and was more of a political struggle than truly a doctrinal one. These debates have been the cause of much confusion in areas of Christian doctrine.

The Names of Christ Indicate His Deity

When the Scriptures refer to any person by name, it indicates much more about the person than just a title or how to refer to them; it indicates their position, personality, and character. Therefore, when comparing the Old and New Testaments, we can see that many names refer to Jesus Christ, and, more than just a myriad of titles, these names are used to display His Deity.

The Names of Christ in the Old Testament

In the Old Testament, we see that future Messiah or Christ is called the "Mighty God" and "Everlasting Father" (Isaiah 9:6). He is called "Lord" in Psalm 110:1. In Isaiah 7:14, He is called, "Immanuel", which is translated "God with us." Jesus is even called "YHWH" or "Jehovah" in Jeremiah 23:6 and Isaiah 40:3—a name that is only used when referring to God. The use of these names all point to the fact that the future Jewish Messiah was to be God Himself.

The reference to Jehovah in Jeremiah 23:5 states: "'Behold, the days are coming, declares the Lord, when I will raise up for David a righteous Branch, and he shall reign as king and deal wisely, and shall execute justice and righteousness in the land.'" To further clarify, the reference of a Branch of David and a King who will prosper and execute judgment is a prophecy of the Messiah's reign; He will reign with righteousness. That is why in verse 6 it says, "And this is the name by which he will be called: 'The LORD [Jehovah] is our righteousness.'" It is not just a proper name, but a description of who He is and how He will reign.

His Names in the New Testament

In the New Testament, the names of Jesus Christ are explicitly of Christ. The New Testament calls Jesus "the Christ" (Matthew 16:16, 20; 23:8; 24:5; Luke 9:20; John 7:26-42; 11:27). This is the Greek word for "anointed," which in Hebrew is the word "Messiah." The definite article before Christ means that He is the One, awaited Messiah prophesied about in the Old Testament.

Scripture refers to Jesus Christ by many different names or titles that refer to His Deity. He is called:

- "God" (John 1:1, 20:24-29; 1 Timothy 1:1; 4:10; Titus 1:3-4; 2:10, 13; 3:4, 6),
- "Lord" (Luke 6:46; 24:34; Mark 2:23-28; John 13:13; Acts 10:36; 26:15; Revelation 19:16),
- "Son of God" (Matthew 16:16; Mark 1:11; 5:7; 15:39; John 10:31-39),
- "Savior" (Titus 1:3-4; 3:4-6),
- "the First and the Last" (Revelation 1:11-17; 2:8; 22:13) (which describes the eternality of Jesus), and
- "I am" (John 8:58-59). (This is the clearest reference to His Deity, since the name "I am" refers to self-existence and is, therefore, a name only used of God.)

Son of God

The phrase "Son of God" is often misunderstood, because people do not take the time to understand the meaning of the term "sonship" in the times and culture of Christ. The word "son," while it can mean offspring, is used most often to refer to one who partakes of, or is identified with, the one to whom he is son. Some examples of this usage are, James and John, who were called the "sons of thunder" (Mark 3:17). Judas was called the, "son of perdition" (John 17:12; 2 Thessalonians 2:3). Also, in Acts 4:36, we see that Joseph is called Barnabas, which means "son of encouragement." It has the idea of essence, not offspring.

I am

When Jesus Christ uses the name "I AM," it is an explicit reference to Deity (John 8:58-59). In the Greek, the phrase for "I AM" is the same as the Hebrew for the name of God in Exodus 3:14, which is often translated YHWH or Jehovah. This is a statement of Deity. It emphasizes the pre-existence and eternality of Jesus. The Jews at the time of Christ understood this because after using this name about Himself in John 8:58, the Jews *"took up stones to throw at Him"* (v. 59) for blasphemy (calling Himself God) (John 10:33).

Lord

Jesus was referred to as "Lord." Some would deny that this title is a reference of Deity because it may be used by man referring to man. While this is true, it is obviously used in reference to Deity as well. It is the context that determines usage. These references are clear statements of the Deity of Christ, especially when used twice; "Lord, Lord" (Luke 6:46). Jesus called Himself Lord several times (Luke 6:46; Mark 2:23-28). Jesus was called Lord by the disciples (Luke 6:46; John 13:13), Mary Magdalene and Mary (Luke 24:34), Peter (Acts 10:36), Paul (Acts 26:15), John (Revelation 19:16), and Thomas called Him "my Lord and my God" (John 20:28).

First and Last

The title "first and last" is used as a title ascribed to YHWH or Jehovah in the Old Testament (Isaiah 44:6; 48:12). This very same title is used of the Lord Jesus Christ by John in His revelation over and over again (Revelation 1:11, 17;

2:8; 2213). The title refers to the attribute of eternality, which is true of God alone.

Savior

In the Old Testament, it is made clear several times that YHWH and YHWH alone is the Savior. God does not share in being the Savior. There is no Savior apart from God. See the following verses:

> *"I, I am the Lord, and besides me there is no savior"* (Isaiah 43:11).

> *"Declare and present your case; let them take counsel together! Who told this long ago? Who declared it of old? Was it not I, the Lord? And there is no other god besides me, a righteous God and a Savior; there is none besides me"* (Isaiah 45:21).

> *But I am the Lord your God from the land of Egypt; you know no God but me, and besides me there is no savior* (Hosea 13:4).

However, in the New Testament, Jesus is called the Savior. Jesus fulfills the title and role that only God can fill. Thus, for Jesus to be called the Savior in the New Testament directly points to His being God from the Old Testament. See the following Scripture references:

> *[...] and at the proper time manifested in his word through the preaching with which I have been entrusted by the command of God our Savior; To Titus, my true child in a common faith: Grace and peace from God the Father and Christ Jesus our Savior* (Titus 1:3-4).

But when the goodness and loving kindness of God our Savior appeared, he saved us, not because of works done by us in righteousness, but according to his own mercy, by the washing of regeneration and renewal of the Holy Spirit, whom he poured out on us richly through Jesus Christ our Savior (Titus 3:4-6).

The Works of Christ Indicate His Deity

The works Jesus Christ did while on earth indicate His Deity. When the Jews challenged Jesus about His Deity, *"Jesus answered them, 'I told you, and you do not believe. The works that I do in my Father's name bear witness about me'"* (John 10:25). We can see here that Jesus clearly stated that His works were a proof of His Deity. He also appealed to His works at other times as proof or witness to His Deity, as is evidenced in His interaction with the blind man:

Jesus answered, "It was not that this man sinned, or his parents, but that the works of God might be displayed in him. We must work the works of him who sent me while it is day; night is coming, when no one can work. As long as I am in the world, I am the light of the world" (John 9:3–5).

In addition, Jesus was involved in works that only God could be involved in doing, such as:

1) Creation
2) Forgiveness of Sins
3) Source of Life
4) Acceptance of Worship
5) Judgment of Mankind

Creation

Creation is a work that God alone can do because it requires an omnipotent and eternal Being. God states that He alone created everything: *"Thus says the Lord, your Redeemer, who formed you from the womb: 'I am the Lord, who made all things, who alone stretched out the heavens, who spread out the earth by myself'"* (Isaiah 44:24).

So if God is the One that created everything and we see that Jesus is clearly credited with creating everything, then it is a simple conclusion that Jesus must be God. There are many claims that Jesus is the Creator of everything. See the following references:

> *All things were made through him, and without him was not any thing made that was made* (John 1:3).

> *Yet for us there is one God, the Father, from whom are all things and for whom we exist, and one Lord, Jesus Christ, through whom are all things and through whom we exist* (1 Corinthians 8:6).

> *[...] and to make all see what is the fellowship of the mystery, which from the beginning of the ages has been hidden in God who created all things through Jesus Christ* (Ephesians 3:9 NKJV).

> *He is the image of the invisible God, the firstborn of all creation. For by him all things were created, in heaven and on earth, visible and invisible, whether thrones or dominions or rulers or authorities—all things were created through him and for him* (Colossians 1:15-16).

But in these last days he has spoken to us by his Son, whom he appointed the heir of all things, through whom also he created the world (Hebrews 1:2).

Forgiveness of Sins

Since we sin against God, then only God can forgive us of sin. Our offense is against God and our forgiveness is only by God. Therefore, since it is Jesus that forgives our sins, then Jesus must be God. Even the Jews at the time recognized the forgiveness of sin as something only God can do:

And behold, some people brought to him a paralytic, lying on a bed. And when Jesus saw their faith, he said to the paralytic, "Take heart, my son; your sins are forgiven." And behold, some of the scribes said to themselves, "This man is blaspheming." But Jesus, knowing their thoughts, said, "Why do you think evil in your hearts? For which is easier, to say, 'Your sins are forgiven,' or to say, 'Rise and walk'? But that you may know that the Son of Man has authority on earth to forgive sins"—he then said to the paralytic—"Rise, pick up your bed and go home" (Matthew 9:2–6).

"Why does this man speak like that? He is blaspheming! Who can forgive sins but God alone?" (Mark 2:7).

Source of Life

Jesus raised two people from the dead and gave them their physical life back after death. In both accounts, the son of the widow at Nain (Luke 7:11-17) and Lazarus (John

11:34–44), Jesus brought someone back to life who was clearly dead and whose body had been prepared for the grave or already placed in the grave. See the account of Lazarus below:

> And he said, "Where have you laid him?" They said to him, "Lord, come and see." Jesus wept. So the Jews said, "See how he loved him!" But some of them said, "Could not he who opened the eyes of the blind man also have kept this man from dying?" Then Jesus, deeply moved again, came to the tomb. It was a cave, and a stone lay against it. Jesus said, "Take away the stone." Martha, the sister of the dead man, said to him, "Lord, by this time there will be an odor, for he has been dead four days." Jesus said to her, "Did I not tell you that if you believed you would see the glory of God?" So they took away the stone. And Jesus lifted up his eyes and said, "Father, I thank you that you have heard me. I knew that you always hear me, but I said this on account of the people standing around, that they may believe that you sent me." When he had said these things, he cried out with a loud voice, "Lazarus, come out." The man who had died came out, his hands and feet bound with linen strips, and his face wrapped with a cloth. Jesus said to them, "Unbind him, and let him go" (John 11:34–44).

Acceptance of Worship

By Accepting Worship, He could not be a mere man

No man is worthy of worship as God. The Jewish leaders knew this and challenged Jesus over this very issue when He claimed to be God. When Jesus claims to be God and accepting of worship as such, they respond by calling it blasphemy: *"The Jews answered him, 'It is not for a good work that we are going to stone you but for blasphemy, because you, being a man, make yourself God'"* (John 10:33).

By Accepting Worship, He could not be an angel

Throughout Scripture it is clear that angels are not worthy of worship as God. There are several times that men attempted to worship angels, and the angels refused it because they knew that it was wrong. Men cannot worship angels as we can see from the following Scripture references:

> *Let no one disqualify you, insisting on asceticism and worship of angels, going on in detail about visions, puffed up without reason by his sensuous mind* (Colossians 2:18).

> *Then I fell down at his feet to worship him, but he said to me, "You must not do that! I am a fellow servant with you and your brothers who hold to the testimony of Jesus. Worship God." For the testimony of Jesus is the spirit of prophecy* (Revelation 19:10).

> *I, John, am the one who heard and saw these things. And when I heard and saw them, I fell down to worship at the feet of the angel who showed them to me, but he said to me, "You must not do that! I am a fellow servant with you and your brothers the prophets, and with those who keep the words of this book. Worship God"* (Revelation 22:8–9).

By Accepting Worship, He Must Be God

Since Jesus knowingly accepted worship as God, we must conclude that He knew He is God. Jesus never refused worship from men. As we can see, Jesus was exalted above men as an equal to God:

> *And those in the boat worshiped him, saying, "Truly you are the Son of God"* (Matthew 14:33).

> *While he blessed them, he parted from them and was carried up into heaven. And they worshiped him and returned to Jerusalem with great joy* (Luke 24:51–52).

> *Therefore God has highly exalted him and bestowed on him the name that is above every name, so that at the name of Jesus every knee should bow, in heaven and on earth and under the earth, and every tongue confess that Jesus Christ is Lord, to the glory of God the Father* (Philippians 2:9–11).

Judgment of Mankind

Jesus clearly claimed to be the judge of all humanity. In order to be the judge of humanity, One must be above humanity. Scripture tells us that Jesus acts as judge—the place of God alone:

> *For the Father judges no one, but has given all judgment to the Son* (John 5:22).

> *And he has given him authority to execute judgment, because he is the Son of Man* (John 5:27).

And he commanded us to preach to the people and to testify that he is the one appointed by God to be judge of the living and the dead (Acts 10:42).

The Attributes of Christ Indicate His Deity

If Jesus Christ is Deity then He should have the attributes of Deity. There are attributes that are only attributed to God. Therefore, if Christ possesses these attributes, it is only because He is God. In the New Testament, we see that Jesus Christ possesses the following attributes of Deity:

- Incomprehensibility
- Sovereignty
- Omniscience
- Omnipotence
- Omnipresence
- Immutability
- Eternality
- Holiness

While possessing the attributes of Deity, Jesus Christ did not necessarily use the attributes of His Deity, but limited Himself by his humanness (Matthew 4:2; Luke 22:43; John 4:6; 19:28). This does not mean that He stopped being God nor was never God, but that somehow He limited Himself to being a man:

Have this mind among yourselves, which is yours in Christ Jesus, who, though he was in the form of God, did not count equality with God a thing to be grasped, but emptied himself, by taking the form of a servant, being born in the likeness of men. And being found in human form, he humbled himself by becoming obedient to the point of death, even death on a cross (Philippians 2:5-8).

Incomprehensibility

One of the first attributes of God to study is His incomprehensibility. God is greater than any human's ability to understand Him. This does not mean that we cannot understand anything about God, but that we can understand only that which He reveals to us. Jesus too is referred to as "unsearchable":

To me, though I am the very least of all the saints, this grace was given, to preach to the Gentiles the unsearchable riches of Christ, [...] and to know the love of Christ that surpasses knowledge, that you may be filled with all the fullness of God (Ephesians 3:8, 19).

Sovereignty

God is the Sovereign of the universe. All things come under the rule of God as the sovereign. As Sovereign, Jesus has the right to rule and judge. That we will all face the judgment seat of Christ is the evidence that He is the Sovereign and Judge. See Romans 14:

But why do you judge your brother? Or why do you show contempt for your brother? For we shall all stand before the judgment seat of Christ. For it is written: "As I live, says the Lord, Every knee shall bow to Me, And every tongue shall confess to God."

12 So then each of us shall give account of himself to God (Romans 14:10-12 NKJV).

Omniscience

No human being knows the mind of another without the other revealing their thoughts. However, that is not so with Jesus. Jesus knew the thoughts of all people. Knowing all things is an attribute called "omniscience." This attribute is uniquely a characteristic of God. No one apart from God can be omniscient. The fact that Jesus was omniscient is evidence that He is God:

> *But Jesus on his part did not entrust himself to them, because he knew all people and needed no one to bear witness about man, for he himself knew what was in man* (John 2:24-25).

> *Now we know that you know all things and do not need anyone to question you; this is why we believe that you came from God." Jesus answered them, "Do you now believe? Behold, the hour is coming, indeed it has come, when you will be scattered, each to his own home, and will leave me alone. Yet I am not alone, for the Father is with me* (John 16:30-32).

Omnipotence

Many falsely think that because Jesus states that He does nothing apart from the will and power of God while on earth means that He is not God. However, the attributes He has cannot be of any man alone. The references to the Son submitting to the Father does not have to do with a lack of attributes of Deity but a submission within the Trinity.

Furthermore, Jesus is not only omnipotent, but He holds all things together:

So Jesus said to them, "Truly, truly, I say to you, the Son can do nothing of his own accord, but only what he sees the Father doing. For whatever the Father does, that the Son does likewise (John 5:19).

For as the Father raises the dead and gives them life, so also the Son gives life to whom he will (John 5:21).

And he is before all things, and in him all things hold together (Colossians 1:17).

Omnipresence

Jesus claims that He is with every believer and that nothing is hidden from Him because all things are open to His eyes. That is an attribute of omnipresence. Omnipresence is another attribute that is only true of God. Thus, since Jesus has this attribute He must be God:

And Jesus came and said to them, "All authority in heaven and on earth has been given to me. Go therefore and make disciples of all nations, baptizing them in the name of the Father and of the Son and of the Holy Spirit, teaching them to observe all that I have commanded you. And behold, I am with you always, to the end of the age" (Matthew 28:18-20).

And no creature is hidden from his sight, but all are naked and exposed to the eyes of him to whom we must give account (Hebrews 4:13).

Immutability

The attribute of immutability means that God cannot change. His attributes and nature are fixed and not changing. This is true only of God, and, as it states in Hebrews, this is true of Jesus: *"Jesus Christ is the same yesterday and today and forever"* (Hebrews 13:8).

Eternal

God and God alone is eternal. Being eternal is specific to being God, because it is not to be created or have a beginning. Unlike all of creation, God has no beginning or end. There are different ways that the eternal nature of Jesus is explained.

One of these ways is that Jesus was in the beginning of creation—meaning that He existed before creation, and thus He is not created*: "In the beginning was the Word, and the Word was with God, and the Word was God"* (John 1:1).

Another is that Jesus claims to be the "I am" as we saw in John 8:58: *"Jesus said to them, 'Truly, truly, I say to you, before Abraham was, I am.'"* And the name for "I am" in the Greek translation of the Hebrew refers to Jehovah God in Exodus 3:14. The importance of this name of God is that it refers to the self-existence nature of God.

Lastly, Jesus claimed to be the "Alpha and Omega," "the Beginning and the End": *"I am the Alpha and the Omega,"* says the Lord God, *"who is and who was and who is to come, the Almighty"* (Revelation 1:8). These terms and others like "the First and the Last" are references to God's eternal nature. The idea behind these terms is that God is eternal, without beginning or end. He is the "first caused Cause" as the philosophers call Him, we can say biblically that He is the "uncaused Cause".

Holiness

Holiness means to be separated. In the case of God He is separated from sin. He cannot sin. Who would know God better than the angels who are or were in His presence?

Angels come in two categories: holy angels and unholy angels, which we call demons. When demons recognize Jesus, they know who He is and refer to Him by the attribute of holiness: *"What have you to do with us, Jesus of Nazareth? Have you come to destroy us? I know who you are—the Holy One of God"* (Mark 1:24).

In conclusion, the two passages which ascribe to Christ one of the greatest statements of Deity is Colossians 2:9, *"For in Him dwells all the fullness of the Godhead bodily"* and Philippians 2:6, *"who, being in the form of God, did not consider it robbery to be equal with God."*

After examining the totality of information on the Deity of Christ, one must say He is one of three things:

Liar	That is, He deceived those who followed Him, telling them He was God.
Lunatic	That is, he was so deluded He did not know what He was saying, claiming to be God.
Lord	He was who He said He was: "The King of Kings and the Lord of Lords."

The Humanity of Christ

While the Deity of Jesus Christ is widely debated, His humanity seems to be widely accepted as fact. However, there are areas of the humanity of Christ that are still misunderstood by different world religions and cults. It is important to look at the purpose, prior existence, evidence, and exaltation of the humanity of Christ.

In the Incarnation, the second person of the Trinity laid aside His right to the full prerogatives of coexistence with God, assumed the place of a Son, and took on an existence appropriate to a servant, while never divesting Himself of His divine attributes (Philippians 2:5-8).

Due to His humanity Jesus can act as the Mediator between God and man (1 Timothy 2:5), the Head of His body the church (Ephesians 1:22; 5:23; Colossians 1:18), and the eternal King, who will reign on the throne of David (Isaiah 9:6; Luke 1:31-33). He is the final Judge of all who fail to place their trust in Him as Lord and Savior (Matthew 25:14-46; Acts 17:30-31).

It is important to note that Jesus had both a physical body and an immaterial spirit because, in the first century, the debate was that Jesus was one or the other, as mutually exclusive options. People had a hard time understanding that Jesus Christ could have two natures: fully God and fully man. It is important that Jesus Christ had two natures in order to be the true Mediator and the true Savior.

The Gnostic thought of the first century was that every good thing was spiritual and everything material was evil. Therefore, they had a problem calling Jesus totally good but also material. They taught that Jesus was a spirit but only appeared to be a man. It is for this reason that the Scripture often states an antichrist is one that does not believe Jesus Christ came in the flesh. See the following passage:

> By this you know the Spirit of God: every spirit that confesses that Jesus Christ has come in the flesh is from God, and every spirit that does not confess Jesus is not from God. This is the spirit of the antichrist, which you heard was coming and now is in the world already (1 John 4:2-3).

The Purpose of the Humanity of Christ

Why did Jesus Christ have to enter into humanity? Being God, Jesus Christ had everything in Heaven where the angels worshiped Him—there is no sin, no sickness, no starvation, and no sorrow. Still, Jesus Christ came to earth to become a man and live among His creation for the purpose of becoming a slave unto His death, burial, and resurrection (Philippians 2:5-8). However, there is more to His purpose than just the cross to the Ascension.

Christ's death, burial, and resurrection provided a sacrifice for sin. Christ's sacrifice was the payment for our sin so that we could be set free. Jesus Christ becomes the fullest revelation of God to man, because *"no one has seen God at any time"* (John 1:18). Now, Jesus Christ acts as the only true Mediator between God and man.

> For our sake he made him to be sin who knew no sin, so that in him we might become the righteousness of God (2 Corinthians 5:21).

But thanks be to God, that you who were once slaves of sin have become obedient from the heart to the standard of teaching to which you were committed, and, having been set free from sin, have become slaves of righteousness (Romans 6:17-18).

But now that you have been set free from sin and have become slaves of God, the fruit you get leads to sanctification and its end, eternal life (Romans 6:22).

For there is one God, and there is one mediator between God and men, the man Christ Jesus (1 Timothy 2:5).

My little children, I am writing these things to you so that you may not sin. But if anyone does sin, we have an advocate with the Father, Jesus Christ the righteous. He is the propitiation for our sins, and not for ours only but also for the sins of the whole world (1 John 2:1-2).

Jesus Christ is the perfect man—the ONLY human to have NEVER sinned. His sinlessness is what makes Him a perfect sacrifice and a perfect example to follow (Philippians 2:5; 1 Peter 2:21). The true mediation of Jesus Christ is possible because He is the ONLY God-man. Yet, He is also a sympathetic High Priest because, being fully human, Jesus can sympathize with humanity.

Being sinful creatures, we can only obtain salvation from God by His acceptance of Jesus as a sacrifice for our sins. If Jesus Christ were not a sinless sacrifice, He would have to pay for His own sins, which would disqualify Him as our substitute. And if He were not also fully human, He would not be able to sympathize with humanity, pleading to the Father on our behalf.

> Therefore he had to be made like his brothers in every respect, so that he might become a merciful and faithful high priest in the service of God, to make propitiation for the sins of the people. For because he himself has suffered when tempted, he is able to help those who are being tempted (Hebrews 2:17-18).

> Since then we have a great high priest who has passed through the heavens, Jesus, the Son of God, let us hold fast our confession. For we do not have a high priest who is unable to sympathize with our weaknesses, but one who in every respect has been tempted as we are, yet without sin. Let us then with confidence draw near to the throne of grace, that we may receive mercy and find grace to help in time of need (Hebrews 4:14-16).

The Prior Existence of the Humanity of Christ

Some falsely teach that Jesus Christ was merely a good man. We have seen in the section on the Deity of Christ that He could not be a just a man, good or otherwise. There are others that teach that Jesus Christ during His time on earth or prior was an angel. His Deity disproves this theory as well. If Jesus Christ was at any point in time an angel, He could never have been the Creator of all things.

Those that see Christ as merely a good man (e.g. the Jewish position) believe Christ came into being at His birth.

Those that see Christ as an angel (e.g. the Jehovah Witness position) believe Christ was created in the form of another being before His birth. The correct view of Jesus Christ prior to His humanity, however, is that He was and is the "I AM" (i.e., God). Scripture clearly shows us that Jesus always was, is, and will be God. As we can see in John 8, Jesus Christ claimed that He was the great "I AM" during Abraham's lifetime:

> Your father Abraham rejoiced that he would see my day. He saw it and was glad." So the Jews said to him, "You are not yet fifty years old, and have you seen Abraham?" Jesus said to them, "Truly, truly, I say to you, before Abraham was, I am." So they picked up stones to throw at him, but Jesus hid himself and went out of the temple (John 8:56-59).

Some see a contradiction with Christ's entrance into humanity because John the Baptist answered that he was not Elijah (John 1:21), yet Jesus Christ stated that John the Baptist was the forerunner (Matthew 11:14; 17:11-13). The solution to this seeming contradiction is that John was one *like* Elijah (Luke 1:17). In order for Christ to sincerely present the kingdom to the Jews, there needed to be a forerunner like Elijah. John unmistakably fulfilled that role. When asked whether he was Elijah, he was rejecting that he was a resurrected Elijah. John had to come as a type of Elijah, but he was not the resurrected Elijah who will come before the second coming to fulfill all the of the prophesies regarding the forerunner to the Messiah.

Another supposed contradiction with Christ's entrance into humanity is with the prophecy of the virgin birth:

"Therefore the Lord himself will give you a sign. Behold, the virgin shall conceive and bear a son, and shall call his name Immanuel" (Isaiah 7:14; c.f. Matthew 1:21-23). The doctrine of the virgin birth has been a point of controversy between conservative evangelicals and liberal theologians for some time. Also, the Roman Catholics add to the controversy by declaring Mary as one who was always a virgin and one who had no need for a Savior.

First, let us look at the events that surrounded the original prophecy. Isaiah was a prophet to Judah from about 740-680 B.C. This particular passage (Isaiah 7) was written around 735 B.C., which is 12 years before northern Israel fell to Assyria. The wicked king Ahaz was being intimidated into submitting to the eventual overthrow of Judah by Assyria. When Ahaz rejected the idea of asking for a sign from God, Isaiah's prophecy reached out to the people of Judah as a promise that the New Testament fulfills for us in the revelation of the Incarnation of Christ (Matthew 1:23).

Matthew, under the inspiration of the Holy Spirit, plainly reveals that the fulfillment of Isaiah's prophecy was the Incarnation of Christ. Liberals and others have argued against the virgin birth and have made claims that this prophecy was already fulfilled during the time of Isaiah. There is some question as to whether this prophecy was fulfilled temporally during Isaiah's day, but there is no question that it was ultimately and completely fulfilled in Christ.

Many liberal and Jewish scholars have attempted to discredit Isaiah 7:14 as a Messianic prophecy by claiming that the Hebrew word *"almah"* simply means a young woman and not a virgin. Previous usages of the word (Genesis 24:43; Exodus 2:8; I Chronicles 15:20; Psalm 46:1; 68:25; Proverbs 30:19; Song of Solomon 1:3; 6:8) all seem to verify the fact that *almah* is used to indicate virginity.

The time element of the fulfillment, as already mentioned, has been a point of difficulty. Was the prophecy fulfilled during the days of Isaiah? If so, the virgin would have been one impregnated by a human father, as opposed to the divine conception of Christ; and the child would have been either Hezekiah (son of Ahaz), Maher-shalal-hash-baz (Isaiah's son), or an unknown child to an unknown virgin. Even if there was a near-term fulfillment of a child born to a virgin, the prophecy still points to a virgin giving birth to the Christ and is the only clear reference we have in Scripture to the prophecy's fulfillment.

The Process of the Humanity of Christ

The process of the Incarnation from the aspect of Jesus is the self-emptying or *kenosis* of Christ (Philippians 2:5-8). This is Christ's voluntary surrender of the exercise of His divine attributes in order to accomplish a number of things:

- To provide a sacrifice for sin (2 Corinthians 5:21).
- To provide an example for our lives (Philippians 2:5).
- To reveal God to man (John 1:18).
- To be a sympathetic High Priest (Hebrews 4:14).

The Evidence of the Humanity of Christ

There are three evidences of the humanity of Christ.

1) He possesses the necessities of humanity.

2) He possesses the names of humanity.
3) He possesses the nature of humanity.

Jesus Christ has the necessities of humanity: a physical body (Hebrews 2:14) and an immaterial soul (Matthew 28:6; Luke 23:46). The reason this is important to note is that the first century Christians were battling the false belief that Jesus Christ did not have a physical body. So when we see a great deal of attention given to Christ's humanity in the later writings, like 1 John, it is because John is trying to combat this false doctrine, not disprove the Deity of Christ that was widely accepted at the time.

Jesus also possesses the name of humanity. He most often called Himself the "Son of Man," emphasizing His humanity (Matthew 8:20; 9:6; 12:8; Mark 8:31, 38; Luke 19:10; John 6:27, 53, 62; 8:28). He was also referred to as a man by others (1 Timothy 2:5). He called Himself a man (John 8:40). Also, He was described in Scripture as having limitations that are common with human nature, such as hunger (Matthew 4:2), thirst (John 19:28), fatigue (John 4:6), exhaustion (Luke 22:43), being bound by time (Mark 11:13), and even experiencing death (John 19:30).

An interesting question to ponder is that since Christ possessed the fullness of humanity, was He able not to sin or was He not able to sin? The answer is that Christ was not able to sin. The union of Deity and humanity is a complete union where neither nature loses something to the other; where both natures retain their attributes while functioning together in Christ.

Remember, Jesus Christ had a perfect human body and never sinned, but that does not mean He was never tempted. In fact, His temptations were far worse than what we suffer. When we are tempted, sometimes we give into the temptation and sin. At that point, the temptation is over. However, Jesus Christ suffered the full extent of every temptation, and yet He never gave into the temptations nor did He sin.

The Exaltation of the Humanity of Christ

The exaltation of the humanity of Jesus Christ deals with the crucifixion and resurrection of Christ. The purpose of the crucifixion of Jesus Christ was accomplished voluntarily and obediently by the second Person of the Godhead for the substitutionary atonement of the sins of the human race. Historically, it is known that Jesus Christ would have died on a cross, not a stake (as Jehovah Witnesses claim), and that it was Jesus Christ on that cross (not Judas as Islam claims).

The resurrection is evidenced by the scriptural testimony (1 Corinthians 15), multitudes of eyewitnesses (vs. 6-7), and historical documentation. Josephus, a Jewish historian for Rome wrote the following:

> Now, there was about this time Jesus, a wise man, if it be lawful to call him a man, for he was a doer of wonderful works—a teacher of such men as receive the truth with pleasure. He drew over to him both many of the Jews, and many of the Gentiles. He was [the] Christ; and when Pilate, at the suggestion of the principal men amongst us, had condemned him

to the cross, those that loved him at the first did not forsake him, for he appeared to them alive again the third day, as the divine prophets had foretold these and ten thousand other wonderful things concerning him; and the tribe of Christians, so named from him, are not extinct at this day.[9]

As we can see, it is important and foundational to note that Jesus was physically born into this world, He physically died, and He physically rose from the dead to ascend into Heaven.

Chapter 5

We believe that people have a sin nature imputed from Adam, which affects every aspect of man, including his will.

Creation of Man

Adam and Eve were directly and immediately created by God on the sixth day of creation, with appearance of age, in God's image and likeness, which means that they were fully formed adults and had the attributes of personality—things like intelligence, emotion, love, etc. Man was created free of sin with a rational nature, intelligence, volition, self-determination, and moral responsibility to God (Genesis 2:7, 15-25; James 3:9). Life of all people begins at conception. The spirit of man does not exist prior to conception (as Mormonism and some others claim).

Man is distinct from animals. Man was made in the image and likeness of God and animals were not. Consequently, man has attributes of personality that animals do not, such as God-consciousness, self-consciousness, world-consciousness, moral decision making, and will. And, even though man has some attributes that animals may also have, man's attributes are superior, such as in intellect, emotion, and communication. As we see in Genesis 1, man was created to have dominion over the animals and the earth:

Then God said, "Let us make man in our image, after our likeness. And let them have dominion over the fish of the sea and over the birds of the heavens and over the livestock and over all the earth and over every creeping thing that creeps on the earth." So God created man in his own image, in the image of God he created him; male and female he created them. And God blessed them. And God said to them, "Be fruitful and multiply and fill the earth and subdue it, and have dominion over the fish of the sea and over the birds of the heavens and over every living thing that moves on the earth" (Genesis 1:26–28).

Humans are distinct from angels in that they are a race and angels are not. This means that humans cannot become angels and angels cannot become humans. Yes, this means that many TV shows and movies have it completely wrong, but people do not become angels after they die. Humans are distinct from both angels and God and will be for all of eternity (Hebrews 1:14; 12:22-24).

People are similar to angels in having a personality, but limited more so in power and abilities. Scripture makes it clear that we, as humans, will judge angels, as we see in 1 Corinthians; therefore, we must conclude that we cannot become angels: *"Do you not know that we are to judge angels? How much more, then, matters pertaining to this life!"* (1 Corinthians 6:3).

Additionally, the author of Hebrews, quoting Psalm 2, points out that mankind is lower than the angels right now:

It has been testified somewhere, "What is man, that you are mindful of him, or the son of man, that you care for him?

You made him for a little while lower than the angels; you have crowned him with glory and honor, putting everything in subjection under his feet."

Now in putting everything in subjection to him, he left nothing outside his control. At present, we do not yet see everything in subjection to him (Hebrews 2:6-8).

God's intention in the creation of man was that man should glorify God, enjoy God's fellowship, live life in the will of God, and, by this, accomplish God's purpose for man in the world:

"I will say to the north, Give up, and to the south, Do not withhold; bring my sons from afar and my daughters from the end of the earth, everyone who is called by my name, whom I created for my glory, whom I formed and made" (Isaiah 43:6-7).

For by him all things were created, in heaven and on earth, visible and invisible, whether thrones or dominions or rulers or authorities—all things were created through him and for him (Colossians 1:16).

"Worthy are you, our Lord and God, to receive glory and honor and power, for you created all things, and by your will they existed and were created" (Revelation 4:11).

God does not call every human a "child of God." Not all people are God's children. The children of God are only those who put their faith in Jesus Christ:

> But to all who did receive him, who believed in his name, he gave the right to become children of God, who were born, not of blood nor of the will of the flesh nor of the will of man, but of God (John 1:12-13).

> And not all are children of Abraham because they are his offspring, but "Through Isaac shall your offspring be named." This means that it is not the children of the flesh who are the children of God, but the children of the promise are counted as offspring (Romans 9:7-8).

Sin Nature

The biggest problem with the doctrine of the sin nature of man is that people do not want to believe it applies to them. People want to believe that they are born spiritually and morally good, or at least spiritually neutral. Christianity can be difficult for some people to accept because of this desire to disbelieve in our own sinful nature. This is the reason that all false religions and cults believe works are necessary in some form or another to achieve salvation. People want to depend on their own "good" works to save themselves.

The sin nature is the reality that sin has been imputed directly from Adam to every individual since Adam (except Jesus Christ, since He was without a human father) (Romans 5:12-19). The imputation of the sin nature means that each person possesses a sinful nature that is passed on from Adam to each generation. By this nature, all people are guilty of sin. The sin nature is inherited and each person is guilty of sin at the point of conception.

This means that every person has a sin nature and is totally depraved in that they lack the proper affection and love toward God and they do sinful/evil things. "Total depravity," more importantly, refers to the fact that the whole of man was corrupted by sin, including man's will. It does not mean that man will be as sinful as possible, for the majority of unsaved people restrain their sinfulness.

Inherited sin addresses the nature of man; whereas imputed sin addresses the reality of that nature imputed to each person from Adam. Adam and Eve became sinners because they sinned, whereas every person afterward sins because they possess a sin nature. After the fall, Adam and Eve committed sin because they now had a sin nature and had become spiritually dead.

In Adam's sin of disobedience to the revealed will and Word of God, man lost his innocence; incurred the penalty of spiritual and physical death; became subject to the wrath of God; and became inherently corrupt and utterly incapable of choosing or doing that which is acceptable to God apart from divine grace (Genesis 2:16-17; 3:1-19; John 3:36; Romans 3:23; 6:23; 1 Timothy 2:13-14; 1 John 1:8). See the following verses:

The natural person does not accept the things of the Spirit of God, for they are folly to him, and he is not able to understand them because they are spiritually discerned (1 Corinthians 2:14).

And you were dead in the trespasses and sins in which you once walked, following the course of this world, following the prince of the power of the air, the spirit that is now at work in the sons of disobedience—among whom we all once lived in the passions of our flesh, carrying out the desires of the body and the mind, and were by nature children of wrath, like the rest of mankind (Ephesians 2:1-3).

With no recuperative powers to enable him to recover himself, man is hopelessly lost. Man's salvation is, thereby, wholly of God's grace through the redemptive work of our Lord Jesus Christ.

Because all of mankind is in Adam, a nature corrupted by Adam's sin has been transmitted to all people of all ages with Jesus Christ being the only exception. As Scripture points out time and again, all people are thus sinners by nature, by choice, and by divine declaration:

The fool says in his heart, "There is no God." They are corrupt, they do abominable deeds; there is none who does good. The Lord looks down from heaven on the children of man, to see if there are any who understand, who seek after God. They have all turned aside; together they have become corrupt; there is none who does good, not even one (Psalm 14:1-3).

The heart is deceitful above all things, and desperately sick; who can understand it? (Jeremiah 17:9).

For if while we were enemies we were reconciled to God by the death of his Son, much more, now that we are reconciled, shall we be saved by his life. More than that, we also rejoice in God through our Lord Jesus Christ, through whom we have now received reconciliation. Therefore, just as sin came into the world through one man, and death through sin, and so death spread to all men because all sinned (Romans 5:10-12).

The results of Adam's sin were a three-fold death:

1. *Physical death*, which is the separation of the body from the spirit, is the particular penalty of imputed sin.
2. *Spiritual death*, which is the separation of the spirit from God (while living on earth), is particular to inherited sin. This is the state in which man is born.
3. *Eternal death*, which is the permanent separation of the body and spirit from any relationship with God, is the particular and final penalty for depravity. Eternal death is a penalty for all unforgiven sin: inherited, imputed, impaired, committed, or omitted. This is the final state of all unbelievers.

Depravity of Man

The depravity of man refers to man being completely and totally corrupted by sin. This depravity includes the will of man (John 8:34). Depravity is any lack of holy affection to God or any bias toward evil. As we have learned, due to imputation of sin, *every* person is a sinner and is depraved.

This passage from Romans 3 makes the human condition very plain:

What then? Are we Jews any better off? No, not at all. For we have already charged that all, both Jews and Greeks, are under sin, as it is written:
*   "None is righteous, no, not one;*
*   no one understands;*
*   no one seeks for God.*
*   All have turned aside; together they have become worthless;*
*   no one does good,*
*   not even one."*
*   "Their throat is an open grave;*
*   they use their tongues to deceive."*
*   "The venom of asps is under their lips."*
*   "Their mouth is full of curses and bitterness."*
*   "Their feet are swift to shed blood;*
*   in their paths are ruin and misery,*
*   and the way of peace they have not known."*
*   "There is no fear of God before their eyes."*

Now we know that whatever the law says it speaks to those who are under the law, so that every mouth may be stopped, and the whole world may be held accountable to God. For by works of the law no human being will be justified in his sight, since through the law comes knowledge of sin. But now the righteousness of God has been manifested apart from the law, although the Law and the Prophets bear witness to it—the righteousness of God through faith in Jesus Christ for all who believe. For

there is no distinction: for all have sinned and fall
short of the glory of God (Romans 3:9-23).

As this chapter makes apparent, the depravity of man is
a total depravity, not partial. But this does not mean that an
unsaved individual has no disposition or tendency to do
good (more on this will be discussed in chapter 7 on
salvation).

Then those who heard it, being convicted by their
conscience, went out one by one, beginning with the
oldest even to the last. And Jesus was left alone, and
the woman standing in the midst (John 8:9 NKJV).

For when Gentiles, who do not have the law, by
nature do what the law requires, they are a law to
themselves, even though they do not have the law
(Romans 2:14).

A depraved sinner is not without some pleasing or
religious qualities (Matthew 23:23; Mark 10:21). A person
as totally depraved is not prone to commit every form of sin
(Matthew 23:23; Romans 2:14; 2 Timothy 3:13), and no
sinner is as intense in sin as he could be (Genesis 15:16;
Matthew 11:24; 2 Timothy 3:13).

Depravity is properly understood that a sinner is
destitute of true love for God (John 5:42), elevates some
lower affection above God (2 Timothy 3:4), prefers self to
God (2 Timothy 3:2), is at enmity with God (Romans 8:7), is
corrupted in every faculty (2 Corinthians 7:1, Ephesians
4:18; Titus 1:15; Hebrews 3:12), can do nothing of which
God can fully approve (Isaiah 64:6; Romans 3:9; 7:18), and

has a pervading tendency toward greater depravity (Romans 7:18, 23).

Total depravity is not total inability. A sinner is restricted but still is sovereign over that which God has placed man over. However, a sinner is limited and unable to change their course of life, prefer God to self, or live above sin; nor is he capable of performing any act fully acceptable to God.

Origin of Sin

The origin of sin was committed by Satan. Scripture does not state when the demons fell, whether it was with Satan or sometime after. We have only two passages that detail the origin of sin by Satan:

"How you are fallen from heaven, O Day Star, son of Dawn! How you are cut down to the ground, you who laid the nations low! You said in your heart, 'I will ascend to heaven; above the stars of God I will set my throne on high; I will sit on the mount of assembly in the far reaches of the north; I will ascend above the heights of the clouds; I will make myself like the Most High.' But you are brought down to Sheol, to the far reaches of the pit. Those who see you will stare at you and ponder over you: 'Is this the man who made the earth tremble, who shook kingdoms, who made the world like a desert and overthrew its cities, who did not let his prisoners go home?' (Isaiah 14:12-17).

Moreover, the word of the Lord came to me: "Son of man, raise a lamentation over the king of Tyre, and say to him, Thus says the Lord God: "You were the signet of perfection, full of wisdom and perfect in beauty. You were in Eden, the garden of God; every precious stone was your covering, sardius, topaz, and diamond, beryl, onyx, and jasper, sapphire, emerald, and carbuncle; and crafted in gold were your settings and your engravings. On the day that you were created they were prepared. You were an anointed guardian cherub. I placed you; you were on the holy mountain of God; in the midst of the stones of fire you walked. You were blameless in your ways from the day you were created, till unrighteousness was found in you. In the abundance of your trade you were filled with violence in your midst, and you sinned; so I cast you as a profane thing from the mountain of God, and I destroyed you, O guardian cherub, from the midst of the stones of fire. Your heart was proud because of your beauty; you corrupted your wisdom for the sake of your splendor. I cast you to the ground; I exposed you before kings, to feast their eyes on you. By the multitude of your iniquities, in the unrighteousness of your trade you profaned your sanctuaries; so I brought fire out from your midst; it consumed you, and I turned you to ashes on the earth in the sight of all who saw you. All who know you among the peoples are appalled at you; you have come to a dreadful end and shall be no more forever" (Ezekiel 28:11-19).

Man's sin was by an historical act that God used to test man (Genesis 3). Satan's sin was the original sin of creation; man's sin was the original sin of the human race (Romans

5:12). Satan's sin was internal, whereas man's sin was influenced by the serpent (Genesis 3). Adam's sin was deliberate, whereas Eve was deceived (1 Timothy 2:14).

The fall of Satan reveals that both man and angels were created with the ability to choose from moral alternatives. A desire to sin arose in Satan. The first sin was rebellion against God's authority and pride in both humans' and angels' potential. Both humans and angels are fully accountable for their own sin. They were not tempted by God, nor did He create sin: *Let no one say when he is tempted, "I am being tempted by God," for God cannot be tempted with evil, and he himself tempts no one* (James 1:13).

Extent of Sin

The extent of sin affects all of creation. We see from Scripture that Eve ate of the fruit of the tree of the knowledge of good and evil but the effect of sin did not occur until Adam partook of it:

> *So when the woman saw that the tree was good for food, and that it was a delight to the eyes, and that the tree was to be desired to make one wise she took of its fruit and ate, and she also gave some to her husband who was with her, and he ate. Then the eyes of both were opened, and they knew that they were naked. And they sewed fig leaves together and made themselves loincloths* (Genesis 3:6-7).

It was not until Adam's sin, that creation began to experience the effects of sin:

And to Adam he said, "Because you have listened to the voice of your wife and have eaten of the tree of which I commanded you, 'You shall not eat of it,' cursed is the ground because of you; in pain you shall eat of it all the days of your life; thorns and thistles it shall bring forth for you; and you shall eat the plants of the field. By the sweat of your face you shall eat bread, till you return to the ground, for out of it you were taken; for you are dust, and to dust you shall return." (Genesis 3:17-19)

After the fall, Adam's sin extended to the entire universe, and it began to physically decay. By the time of the flood, the full effects of sin on creation were experienced. The extent of sin in angels is seen in that they are confirmed in holiness or sinfulness for all eternity. The extent of sin in man is revealed in the depravity of man.

The idea that the universe is decaying has been proven in science and is known as the Second Law of Thermal Dynamics. This law states that all energy in the known universe is in a consist state of decay or entropy. Scripture not only supports this law but also states that a day is coming when the curse on the universe will be removed:

For the creation waits with eager longing for the revealing of the sons of God. For the creation was subjected to futility, not willingly, but because of him who subjected it, in hope that the creation itself will be set free from its bondage to corruption and obtain the freedom of the glory of the children of God. For we know that the whole creation has been groaning together in the pains of childbirth until now (Romans 8:19–22).

Imputation of Sin

Imputation of sin is the inheriting of the sin nature directly from Adam to his offspring. This one act caused a sin nature in every man, even before there was a written law to explain the penalties. The immediate result of that one act of sin was death—physical, spiritual, and ultimately eternal. This death has been passed on to everyone from generation to generation, even to those not conscious.

Ultimately, for this one act of sin, there was also one act of righteousness by Christ—one that remedies the act of Adam. The sin of Adam was a real event and test in history, not a mythical account. In Romans 5, we can see how the sin of Adam contrasts and compares to the salvation of Christ. This passage reveals the similarities and differences between the two historical events:

Therefore, just as sin came into the world through one man, and death through sin, and so death spread to all men because all sinned—for sin indeed was in the world before the law was given, but sin is not counted where there is no law. Yet death reigned from Adam to Moses, even over those whose sinning was not like the transgression of Adam, who was a type of the one who was to come.

But the free gift is not like the trespass. For if many died through one man's trespass, much more have the grace of God and the free gift by the grace of that one man Jesus Christ abounded for many. And the free gift is not like the result of that one man's sin. For the judgment following one trespass brought condemnation, but the free gift following many trespasses brought justification. For if, because of one man's trespass, death reigned through that one man, much more will those who receive the abundance of grace and the free gift of righteousness reign in life through the one man Jesus Christ.

Therefore, as one trespass led to condemnation for all men, so one act of righteousness leads to justification and life for all men. For as by the one man's disobedience the many were made sinners, so by the one man's obedience the many will be made righteous (Romans 5:12–19).

The parallels between Adam and Christ are seen in the "oneness." The result of Adam's sin was both physical and spiritual death. The "oneness" is revealed in the one sinful act of Adam and the one righteous act of Christ. The sin nature extends to all people, except Christ. Sin was brought into the world by one sinful act, not multiple acts. Thus, Christ's death was one act for one act, not one act for many acts. Therefore, Christ died by one act for all of sin, not for many sins. We do not repent of sins (plural) because that would be works-based and a works righteousness system. Instead, we repent of sin, the whole of our sin nature or pride and selfishness.

Due to Adam's one sin, all humans are rightly judged for imputed sin. It is deserved and applies to all. However, grace is not extended to all and is completely and totally unmerited by humans. Because of this, not all men are in Christ, but all men are born in Adam. In other words, all humans are born into Adam (sin nature) but only some are born again into Christ (salvation through grace). The result of being in Adam is condemnation, but the imputation of righteousness by being in Christ is redemption. Those in Adam have a certain death, both physical and spiritual. However, those in Christ do not have a spiritual death any longer and may even avoid the physical death in the rapture (though not all Christians believe in the doctrine of the rapture).

Now that we see the parallels and differences, we can see that there is a similarity and, even more so, a superiority of Christ over Adam. There is a similarity to all being "in Adam" and those "in Christ": the one act of Adam and one act of Christ; the union with Adam and those in union with Christ. The superiority lies within the *nature* of the one act of Christ—an act that has the power to impute His righteousness to those who are in Adam. Christ's one act is the *remedy* for the result of Adam's one act.

The superiority can also be seen in the contrast between Adam and Christ: Adam was disobedient while Christ was obedient; Adam's act was imputed to all people while Christ's righteous act is imputed to few people; Adam's act has the involvement and participation of each person but Christ's act has the involvement and participation of only Christ, and not any man.

Another important note about the similarity in "oneness" between Adam and Christ is in a "natural oneness" verses a "spiritual oneness." Because Adam's is a natural union and Christ's is a spiritual one, all people are in Adam and only some people are in Christ. The union with Adam is immediate at conception—an inescapable part of being born into this world—and the union with Christ is conditional based upon faith and regeneration. All suffer through Adam because of his act, but only Christ suffered by His act.

No one can escape the imputation of sin, but few receive the imputation of righteousness. Therefore, all men are deserving of the imputation of sin and its judgment, but none are deserving of the grace of God. While all sin is merited, grace is completely unmerited.

Answering Objections

There are some objections that are often raised on the topic of sin—questions that can be easily answered.

First, there is the objection that there is no sin prior to "consciousness." However, most sin is of nature rather than deliberate. For example, the first act of an infant is a self-focused desire for milk which results in crying. That cry for milk is an act of selfishness, which is all an infant knows. Thus, the very first act of an infant is selfish, although the infant is not conscious of sin. In addition, we know from first-hand experience that nobody has ever had to teach a child to sin. At the earliest age, children will test their parents with what they know is wrong. As soon as a child can speak, they start lying. These are examples of sins from a sin nature, meaning that they are known prior to "consciousness."

The second objection is that we cannot be responsible for what Adam did. However, we are responsible for what we do. Because of Adam, we have a sin nature, and, therefore, we sin. It is our sin, then, for which we are responsible to God.

This is often followed by the objection that we cannot repent of Adam's sin. However, it is because of sin (singular) and not sins (plural) that we need to repent. Can we be guilty of all of Adam's sins? Adam made one choice that gave him, and every person after him, a sin nature, making us, not guilty of Adam's sins, but guilty of our own sins.

Although Adam's one sinful act brought about a sin nature, in that all mankind sins, one righteous act of Christ brought about the availability for any to have His righteousness imputed to them. Where the sin nature is once to all, righteousness is once to few.

Chapter 6

Creation, Fall, and Promise

We believe that Adam and Eve were real, historical people who were created in the Garden of Eden about 6,000 years ago.

T he following chapter is adapted from the book *On the Origin* of *Kinds* by Dr. Anthony Silvestro and John Eckel (available at http://OnTheOriginOfKinds.com):

Genesis: The First Three Chapters

The first three chapters of Genesis cover:

1. God's perfect creation (Genesis 1 and Genesis 2),

2. the fall (Genesis 3),

3. the curse over all creation (Genesis 3), and

4. God's plan of redemption: the promise of the Savior (Genesis 3:15).

In Genesis 1, God created everything over six, 24-hour, literal days. Notice that I did not say "solar days." The sun was not created until day four. Many people wrongly object to the idea of God creating within six, 24-hour, literal days because there was no sun present in days one through three. Therefore, they believe that the creation account cannot be literal. However, the absence of the sun during this time frame is not actually a problem because "one day" is defined as "one rotation of the earth on its axis." The length of a day has nothing to do with the sun—it just so happens that the sun *appears* to rise and set each day.

At the end of day six, God deemed His creation to be perfect: "*And God saw everything that he had made, and, behold, it was very good. And there was evening and there was morning, the sixth day*" (Genesis 1:31). The word "good" is used six times in Genesis 1, and, at the end of His work on day six, while looking over His entire creation, God said "good" for the seventh time: "*[...] It was very good.*" This perfect creation is also described in many verses of the Bible, such as in reference to God creating a new Garden of Eden at the consummation and in the following verses from Revelation 21:

> *Then I saw a new heaven and a new earth, for the first heaven and the first earth had passed away, and the sea was no more. And I saw the holy city, new Jerusalem, coming down out of heaven from God, prepared as a bride adorned for her husband. And I heard a loud voice from the throne saying, "Behold, the dwelling place of God is with man. He will dwell with them, and they will be his people, and God himself will be with them as their God. He will wipe away every tear from their eyes, and death shall be no more, neither shall there be mourning, nor crying, nor pain anymore, for the former things have passed away." And he who was seated on the throne said, "Behold, I am making all things new."*

Also he said, "Write this down, for these words are trustworthy and true" (Revelation 21:1-5).

In Genesis 2, a detailed account of day six, we see the one main command given to Adam: *"And the Lord God commanded the man, saying, 'You may surely eat of every tree of the garden, but of the tree of the knowledge of good and evil you shall not eat, for in the day that you eat of it you shall surely die'"* (Genesis 2:16-17). It should be noted here that the command was not given to Eve, as she was not yet created.

It is important to understand that this command did not mean that Adam would immediately drop dead physically. What it did mean is that Adam would die both spiritually (immediately) and physically (later). (We will see Biblical proof of these statements later in the chapter.)

In Genesis 3, we get a correct understanding of why bad things are in the world: it comes as a result of "the fall." We see this play out in the first several verses: *"Now the serpent was more crafty than any other beast of the field that the Lord God had made. He said to the woman, 'Did God actually say, "You shall not eat of any tree in the garden"?'"* (Genesis 3:1).

This verse gives us the first sighting of Satan in the Bible. He came in the form of a serpent and challenged God by asking Eve a question. Notice how Satan used God's Word (the command given to Adam in Genesis 2) but twisted it slightly. This is reminiscent of the false teachers of today, such as the prosperity gospel teachers, Word of Faith (WOF) preachers, and those of the New Apostolic Reformation (NAR).

In these two verses, we see Eve's response to the serpent: *"And the woman said unto the serpent, 'We may eat of the fruit of the trees in the garden, but God said, "You shall not eat of the fruit of the tree that is in the midst of the garden, neither shall you touch it, lest you die"'"* (Genesis 3:2-3). She also used God's Word to respond—and also got it wrong.

As stated earlier, the original command was given to Adam only, but, clearly, Eve knew of this command. Something must have gone awry in the communication of God's Word from Adam to Eve. One of the following things must have happened (though we cannot know which based upon Scripture): Adam did not teach his wife correctly regarding God's Word; Eve did not listen well to correct teaching from Adam and did not learn it; or Eve knew the correct teaching and did not articulate it correctly to the Serpent.

Next, we see the answer given by the Serpent: *"But the serpent said to the woman, 'You will not surely die. For God knows that when you eat of it your eyes will be opened, and you will be like God, knowing good and evil'"* (Genesis 3:4-5). The serpent challenged God and His Word in his response to Eve. He also told Eve that she and Adam could be like God Himself, knowing good and evil. What did Eve do when given the ability to be like God? How did she handle the temptation?

So when the woman saw that the tree was good for food, and that it was a delight to the eyes, and that the tree was to be desired to make one wise, she took of its fruit and ate, and she also gave some to her husband who was with her, and he ate. Then the eyes of both were opened, and they knew that they were naked. And they sewed fig leaves together and made themselves loincloths (Genesis 3:6-7).

As their eyes were suddenly opened, the world, starting with them, was exposed to evil. They immediately died spiritually. The first thing they noticed was that they were naked! Of course, they were naked all along, but now they knew the evil part of their nakedness. This is exactly why Genesis 2 ends with the following verse that seems like it doesn't really flow with the rest of the chapter: *"And the man and his wife were both naked and were not ashamed"* (Genesis 2:25). While this verse seems to be tacked onto the end of Genesis 2 and not belong there, its placement makes sense in the context of Genesis 3! Their reaction was to immediately sew fig leaves to cover their nakedness and shame, and they attempted to hide from God. This probably sounds familiar, as we humans all tend to attempt to hide when we sin. What happened next was that God confronted Adam with his sin:

And they heard the sound of the Lord God walking in the garden in the cool of the day, and the man and his wife hid themselves from the presence of the Lord God among the trees of the garden. But the Lord God called to the man and said to him, "Where are you?" And he said, "I heard the sound of you in the garden, and I was afraid, because I was naked, and I hid myself." He said, "Who told you that you were naked? Have you eaten of the tree of which I commanded you not to eat?" (Genesis 3:8-11).

Spiritual death happened immediately to Adam and Eve, and the promise of an eventual physical death would soon follow. The whole world would start to decay as a result of this original sin. We will see the Biblical proof of this next.

Genesis: The Fall and the Promise

Because of this original sin, we now see all the bad entering the world, including death, disease, suffering, extinction, thorns and thistles, and so on. *All* of creation was affected:

For the creation was subjected to futility, not willingly, but because of him who subjected it, in hope that the creation itself will be set free from its bondage to corruption and obtain the freedom of the glory of the children of God. For we know that the whole creation has been groaning together in the pains of childbirth until now. And not only the creation, but we ourselves, who have the firstfruits of the Spirit, groan inwardly as we wait eagerly for adoption as sons, the redemption of our bodies (Romans 8:20-23).

The next thing that we see is the blame game: Adam blamed God for giving him Eve, and Eve pointed her finger at the serpent for his deception: *"The man said, 'The woman whom you gave to be with me, she gave me fruit of the tree, and I ate.' Then the Lord God said to the woman, 'What is this that you have done?' The woman said, 'The serpent deceived me, and I ate'"* (Genesis 3:12-13).

God then began to curse His creation, starting with the serpent: *"The Lord God said to the serpent, 'Because you have done this, cursed are you above all livestock and above all beasts of the field; on your belly you shall go, and dust you shall eat all the days of your life'"* (Genesis 3:14). Furthermore, God continued to curse His creation, next speaking about humanity:

1. He cursed the woman by multiplying pain during childbirth (Genesis 3:16).

2. He cursed the relationship between husband and wife in marriage, ruining the original perfect harmony. The woman will try to gain power and usurp authority over her husband, but the husband will attempt to dominate her (Genesis 3:16).

3. He cursed the ground and Adam. Thorns and thistles would now appear in the garden between the plants and trees from which they would eat. Work, which God did intend for Adam in Genesis 2, would now be hard and laborious (Genesis 3:17-19).

The last part of the curse is shown in the following verses; it is clear that physical death would be the end result of original sin:

"By the sweat of your face you shall eat bread, till you return to the ground, for out of it you were taken; for you are dust, and to dust you shall return"

[...] Then the Lord God said, "Behold, the man has become like one of us in knowing good and evil. Now, lest he reach out his hand and take also of the tree of life and eat, and live forever—" therefore the Lord God sent him out from the garden of Eden to work the ground from which he was taken. He drove out the man, and at the east of the Garden of Eden he placed the cherubim and a flaming sword that turned every way to guard the way to the tree of life (Genesis 3:19,22-24).

We have seen how God cursed His creation as a result of original sin, and the bookend verses of this curse are Genesis 3:7 (immediate spiritual death) and Genesis 3:19 (an impending, certain physical death). However, in the middle of these verses is something so glorious! God gives us the promise of the coming Savior—the first prophecy of the Lord Jesus Christ: *"And I will put enmity between thee and the woman, and between thy seed and her seed; it shall bruise thy head, and thou shalt bruise his heel"* (Genesis 3:15 KJV). We see here that the Savior would come from the seed of the woman, which is what makes the genealogies so important throughout the Bible!

Now, with the shame of nakedness and the promise of the Savior, yet another important concept is born here in Genesis 3 that lasts the entirety of the Old Testament. It is the use of animal sacrifice (bloodshed) to temporarily cover sin: *"And the Lord God made for Adam and for his wife garments of skins and clothed them"* (Genesis 3:21). While Adam and Eve covered their shame with fig leaves (Genesis 3:7), God demanded blood.

The first animal sacrifice occurred in the Garden of Eden, with God Himself killing the first animal and using the skins of the bloodshed animal to cover their sin. This pattern is repeated throughout the Old Testament as the Israelites were instructed to slay a first-born, unblemished animal to be a temporary cover for their sin. These sacrifices foreshadowed the perfect and complete sacrifice of Jesus Christ—the unblemished, first-born, Lamb of God—who took away the sins of the world. Hebrews 9:22 tells us that *"[...] without the shedding of blood there is no forgiveness of sins."*

It is easy to see why a literal interpretation of the beginning of Genesis is vital to a correct understanding of the rest of the Bible. God's plan of redemption is based on what happened in Genesis. Considering all of this, something else should be very apparent. The Bible teaches that death is only a result of sin. Because death is the result of sin, death could not have been present before Adam's original sin. Therefore, the world, and all that is in it, could not have just evolved because evolution requires death to have always been present!

We believe salvation is by grace alone, through faith in Christ alone, with no element of works to merit righteousness.

Salvation is wholly of God alone, by grace alone, through faith alone, by the redemption of Jesus Christ alone, and through the merit of His shed blood. It is not based on human merit, works, genealogy, or will. See the following passages:

> *But to all who did receive him, who believed in his name, he gave the right to become children of God, who were born, not of blood nor of the will of the flesh nor of the will of man, but of God* (John 1:12-13).

> *In him we have redemption through his blood, the forgiveness of our trespasses, according to the riches of his grace* (Ephesians 1:7).

> *For by grace you have been saved through faith. And this is not your own doing; it is the gift of God, not a result of works, so that no one may boast. For we are his workmanship, created in Christ Jesus for good works, which God prepared beforehand, that we should walk in them* (Ephesians 2:8-10).

> *But when the goodness and loving kindness of God our Savior appeared, he saved us, not because of works done by us in righteousness, but according to*

his own mercy, by the washing of regeneration and renewal of the Holy Spirit, whom he poured out on us richly through Jesus Christ our Savior, so that being justified by his grace we might become heirs according to the hope of eternal life (Titus 3:4-7).

[...] knowing that you were ransomed from the futile ways inherited from your forefathers, not with perishable things such as silver or gold, but with the precious blood of Christ, like that of a lamb without blemish or spot (1 Peter 1:18-19).

It is this one doctrine that makes Christianity different from ALL others. Christians believe there is NO work from man that can save a person, nor can they assist God in their salvation. The doctrine of salvation is the one doctrine that is both eternally important and unique to Christianity. All religions can be classified into two categories: the merit of man (works salvation) or the grace of God (imputed righteousness). In other words, salvation is either by man's works of righteousness or God's works of righteousness, but it cannot be both. All religions except Christianity fit into the merit or works-of-man category.

An objective manner to determine which religion is true and of God is to evaluate religions based on this principle of righteousness: whether it is by human effort or divine effort. Mankind will always add praise to themselves or to anything they create. Therefore, any manmade religion will have an element of human effort necessary to get right with God. Christianity stands alone as the only religion that states that God does all the work in justification.

Salvation is often confusing because people use the word "salvation" to mean many different things. There are several aspects covered by the word "salvation." For example, it can refer to the entire salvation process from the convicting work of the Holy Spirit to the glorification of man in Heaven. It can also be used to refer specifically to the act of regeneration or to speak of someone coming to faith. It is really this broad use of the word "salvation" that causes much of the confusion.

Salvation is a process that starts with the Holy Spirit convicting the heart of a sinner and drawing them to repentance, and it ends with a believer's glorification upon entrance into Heaven. Many have a problem because they do not understand that the Holy Spirit convicts sinners prior to the specific act of salvation—meaning that He convicts prior to regeneration or justification. A sinner can reject or resist the convicting work of the Holy Spirit. (This is not the same as resisting the grace of salvation.)

The specific act of salvation is that point in time when someone goes from being an enemy of God to a child of God. The specific act of salvation involves many simultaneous aspects of doctrine. These many aspects of salvation include: regeneration, conversion, repentance, faith, justification, adoption, Spirit baptism, and indwelling of the Holy Spirit. These aspects occur simultaneously and immediately at the point of salvation.

In addition, there are ongoing aspects of salvation that start at the point of salvation and continue until glorification, including sanctification, perseverance, and the filling of the Holy Spirit. The indwelling of the Holy Spirit is mentioned both as a simultaneous event (baptism of the Spirit) and continual event (filling of the Spirit) because, at the point of salvation, we are controlled by the Holy Spirit to be regenerated, but it is also an on-going process called sanctification. Sanctification is the process where the Holy Spirit makes believers more and more into Christ-likeness; whereas the baptism of the Holy Spirit happens only once at the point of salvation. The final act of salvation is glorification in heaven when believers receive a sinless existence (body and spirit).

Therefore, salvation has a past (regeneration), present (sanctification), and future (glorification) aspect. These three aspects must be clearly understood and differentiated. Most cults and false teachings tend to confuse the aspects of regeneration and sanctification. This confusion is seen when people talk of works being necessary for salvation (regeneration). In actuality, works are part of sanctification, which follows regeneration and is not part of regeneration itself.

It is also important to understand that there is no chronological order to the aspects of salvation (regeneration). A person does not believe at one point in time and then later, at another point in time, get regenerated; nor does God regenerate a person at a point in time so that they can believe at a later point in time. These acts are simultaneous. If someone makes the order of salvation a chronological issue, they are forced to accept that a person can be either an unregenerate believer or a regenerate unbeliever, and neither is possible. Humans may not have the ability to understand how these acts can be simultaneous, but Scripture teaches that God is completely sovereign in the salvation of humans, and yet humans still have a responsibility (Romans 9-10).

When considering the many different aspects of salvation, it is good to think in terms of the following four areas:

1. Where does the activity take place, on earth or in Heaven?
2. Is the activity for all believers of all time or only for church age believers?
3. Who is the agent of activity, God or man?
4. What is the type of activity, one of experiential or judicial?

These areas may help us to see the multiple dimensions of the terms used for salvation. The chart below should be of assistance in showing the different facets of salvation:

	Area of Activity	Dispensation of Activity	Agent of Activity	Type of Activity
Election	Heaven	All	Divine	Judicial
Regeneration	Earth		Divine	Experiential
Conversion (Repentance and Faith)	Earth	All	Human	Experiential
Justification	Heaven	All	Divine	Judicial
Adoption	Earth and Heaven	All	Divine	Judicial
Spirit Baptism	Earth and Heaven	Church	Divine	Judicial
Indwelling	Earth	Church	Divine	Experiential
Sanctification	Earth	All	Divine	Experiential
Perseverance	Earth	All	Human	Experiential
Glorification	Heaven	All	Divine	Experiential

Election

Election is the act of God by which, before the foundation of the world, He chose in Christ those whom He graciously regenerates, saves, and sanctifies. See the following references:

> And we know that for those who love God all things work together for good, for those who are called according to his purpose. For those whom he foreknew he also predestined to be conformed to the image of his Son, in order that he might be the firstborn among many brothers. And those whom he predestined he also called, and those whom he called he also justified, and those whom he justified he also glorified (Romans 8:28–30).

> [...] even as he chose us in him before the foundation of the world, that we should be holy and blameless before him. In love he predestined us for adoption to himself as sons through Jesus Christ, according to the purpose of his will, to the praise of his glorious grace, with which he has blessed us in the Beloved. In him we have redemption through his blood, the forgiveness of our trespasses, according to the riches of his grace, which he lavished upon us, in all wisdom and insight making known to us the mystery of his will, according to his purpose, which he set forth in Christ as a plan for the fullness of time, to unite all things in him, things in heaven and things on earth. In him we have obtained an inheritance, having been predestined according to the purpose of him who

works all things according to the counsel of his will (Ephesians 1:4–11).

But we ought always to give thanks to God for you, brothers beloved by the Lord, because God chose you as the firstfruits to be saved, through sanctification by the Spirit and belief in the truth (2 Thessalonians 2:13).

Therefore I endure everything for the sake of the elect, that they also may obtain the salvation that is in Christ Jesus with eternal glory (2 Timothy 2:10).

Peter, an apostle of Jesus Christ, To those who are elect exiles of the Dispersion in Pontus, Galatia, Cappadocia, Asia, and Bithynia, according to the foreknowledge of God the Father, in the sanctification of the Spirit, for obedience to Jesus Christ and for sprinkling with his blood: May grace and peace be multiplied to you (1 Peter 1:1–2).

Some may argue that election is the first step in the process of salvation. To an extent this is correct and also incorrect. When discussing election it must be understood that it is a doctrine of God, who is eternal and not bound by time. Therefore, God uses phrases like *"elect before the foundation of the earth"* (Ephesians 1:4) to explain to humans something that humans cannot comprehend. Election occurs outside of time because it is of God. Therefore, it cannot truly be placed in a chronological order without violating the nature of God.

Sovereign election does not contradict or negate human responsibility to repent and trust Christ as Savior and Lord.

Some people make a false accusation that, if God is sovereign, then He must take pleasure in the death and punishment of the wicked. This claim often comes from professing atheists. However, any parent knows the important of punishment and the pain that comes with the punishment. God makes it clear that He takes no joy in the punishment of the wicked, but, as a just judge, He must do what is right. As we can see from Scripture, the individual bears the responsibility of their actions, including their rejection of God:

> Have I any pleasure in the death of the wicked, declares the Lord God, and not rather that he should turn from his way and live? (Ezekiel 18:23).

> "For I have no pleasure in the death of anyone, declares the Lord God; so turn, and live." (Ezekiel 18:32)

> Say to them, As I live, declares the Lord God, I have no pleasure in the death of the wicked, but that the wicked turn from his way and live; turn back, turn back from your evil ways, for why will you die, O house of Israel? (Ezekiel 33:11).

> "Whoever believes in him is not condemned, but whoever does not believe is condemned already, because he has not believed in the name of the only Son of God. And this is the judgment: the light has come into the world, and people loved the darkness rather than the light because their works were evil" (John 3:18–19).

Whoever believes in the Son has eternal life; whoever does not obey the Son shall not see life, but the wrath of God remains on him (John 3:36).

Yet you refuse to come to me that you may have life (John 5:40).

What if God, desiring to show his wrath and to make known his power, has endured with much patience vessels of wrath prepared for destruction, in order to make known the riches of his glory for vessels of mercy, which he has prepared beforehand for glory (Romans 9:22–23).

[...] and with all wicked deception for those who are perishing, because they refused to love the truth and so be saved. Therefore God sends them a strong delusion, so that they may believe what is false, in order that all may be condemned who did not believe the truth but had pleasure in unrighteousness (2 Thessalonians 2:10–12).

The Spirit and the Bride say, "Come." And let the one who hears say, "Come." And let the one who is thirsty come; let the one who desires take the water of life without price (Revelation 22:17).

Nevertheless, because sovereign grace includes the means of receiving the gift of salvation as well as the gift itself, sovereign election will result in what God determines. All whom the Father calls to Himself will come in faith, and all who come in faith the Father will receive:

All that the Father gives me will come to me, and whoever comes to me I will never cast out. For I have come down from heaven, not to do my own will but the will of him who sent me. And this is the will of him who sent me, that I should lose nothing of all that he has given me, but raise it up on the last day. For this is the will of my Father, that everyone who looks on the Son and believes in him should have eternal life, and I will raise him up on the last day (John 6:37–40).

No one can come to me unless the Father who sent me draws him. And I will raise him up on the last day (John 6:44).

And when the Gentiles heard this, they began rejoicing and glorifying the word of the Lord, and as many as were appointed to eternal life believed (Acts 13:48).

Draw near to God, and he will draw near to you. Cleanse your hands, you sinners, and purify your hearts, you double-minded (James 4:8).

The unmerited favor that God grants to totally depraved sinners is not related to any initiative of their own part, nor to God's anticipation of what they might do by their own will, but is solely of His sovereign grace and mercy. God does not look down the tunnels of time to see the response of people and then make a decision as if He was a being bound by time. God is eternal. In fact, for those who struggle with this, the clearest argument Paul makes is in Philippians 1:29 where he makes the point that suffering is granted to the believer just as believing was granted to the believer: *"For it has been granted to you that for the sake of Christ you should not only believe in him but also suffer for his sake."* Therefore, even our belief is granted to us by God (Ephesians 1:4-7; Titus 3:4-7; 1 Peter 1:2).

Election should not be looked upon as based merely on abstract sovereignty. God is truly sovereign, but He exercises this sovereignty in harmony with His other attributes, especially His omniscience, justice, holiness, wisdom, grace, and love. Paul makes this argument in Romans as he compares the twin brothers Esau and Jacob. Note that Paul is not using them as a type of the Gentile and Jewish nations but as two individual people; thus, this election is not corporate but personal:

> *[...] though they were not yet born and had done nothing either good or bad—in order that God's purpose of election might continue, not because of works but because of him who calls—she was told, "The older will serve the younger." As it is written, "Jacob I loved, but Esau I hated." What shall we say then? Is there injustice on God's part? By no means! For he says to Moses, "I will have mercy on whom I have mercy, and I will have compassion on whom I have compassion." So then it depends not on human will or exertion, but on God, who has mercy* (Romans 9:11–16).

This sovereignty will always exalt the will of God in a manner totally consistent with His character as revealed in the life of our Lord Jesus Christ. This is one of the things you will see with every false, man-made religion, they will exalt mankind and their works. The Bible exalts God and His work:

> At that time Jesus declared, "I thank you, Father, Lord of heaven and earth, that you have hidden these things from the wise and understanding and revealed them to little children; yes, Father, for such was your gracious will. All things have been handed over to me by my Father, and no one knows the Son except the Father, and no one knows the Father except the Son and anyone to whom the Son chooses to reveal him. Come to me, all who labor and are heavy laden, and I will give you rest (Matthew 11:25–28).

> [...] who saved us and called us to a holy calling, not because of our works but because of his own purpose and grace, which he gave us in Christ Jesus before the ages began (2 Timothy 1:9).

The following excerpts are from a message entitled "God's Sovereignty and Human Responsibility in Salvation" on Romans 9-10 and can be found in its entirety at strivingforeternity.org:

> Some may argue that Romans 9 is not discussing God's personal election of men, but instead God's sovereign election of the nation of Israel. Although, this clearly fits in the context of the passage of Romans 9–11, Paul is using this illustration of Israel to apply to the personal election of men, both Jew and Gentile. Paul's main point in this passage is that

individuals, both Jew and Gentile, can be children of the promise.

Paul is making the argument that people are not children of God just because they are born of the lineage of Abraham. A child of God is one who has faith in God (v. 8). Abraham had at least eight children named in the Bible (Genesis 25:2). Therefore, Isaac could not claim to be the only born son of Abraham. Yet, Isaac was not even the first-born son of Abraham. Ishmael was the first-born. Paul's argument of God's sovereignty in election is that the promise did not come from the first-born son but instead from the son of the promise, the second born son.

[...] The one thing that MUST be remembered in discussing God's sovereignty is that God is God. It sounds simple, but think about it. It is God who formed the universe. It is God who made everything out of nothing. It is God who made the earth. It is God who gives life. It is God who shows mercy and compassion on whom He chooses (v. 15). We cannot separate the fact that God as God has the right and the authority to create His creation any way He wants. The universe is His to control and so are we. God formed everything out of nothing, from the smallest element of an atom to the entirety of the universe. If there is one atom in the entire universe that is outside God's control then He is not sovereign. Nothing is outside His control. Verse 16 says, *"So then it is not of him who wills, nor of him who runs, but of God who shows mercy."* Paul goes so far as to state that God is not only righteous in electing some for mercy, but He is righteous in hardening the heart of others, like the Pharaoh of Egypt during the time of Moses. This may seem hard to understand, but if one does not understand what God, through Paul, is stating here, they will never properly understand God's sovereignty. We need to start at the beginning.

Due to Adam's sin in the Garden of Eden when he attempted to become the sovereign of the world, humanity has fallen. This fall has caused ALL of humanity to be conceived with a sinful nature, whether we like it or not. The sinful nature of man means that we ALL sin and are sinners. Therefore, we are ALL under the judgment of God. Every person born into this world starts out evil and is destined for judgment and hell.

The reason people would ask Paul if God is unjust is because they believe that they are naturally good, or at best neutral toward God. However, we are God's enemies (Romans 1:30; 8:7; James 4:4). Every person's starting point in life is not Heaven, it is Hell. Therefore, it is not God's justice that should be questioned when we discuss His election, but His mercy.

That is why Paul quotes from the Old Testament to say that God has the right to show mercy on whomever He wants. God does not damn people to Hell; they are already on their way there the second they are conceived. The fact that God shows mercy on anyone is the amazing thing. We should ask how God can show mercy on sinners, not question His justice as if He is somehow obligated to show mercy to all people. If you have followed along with me, you should be asking, as Paul expects to be asked, *"You will say to me then, 'Why does [God] still find fault? For who has resisted His will?'"* (v. 19).

If God is the One to show mercy and it is completely His decision, then how can people be held responsible? After all, no one can resist God's will. That is the thought. Many people stumble over this thought. Most people end up deducing one of two outcomes from this passage: either salvation is all of God and man has no responsibility, or it is ultimately man's choice and God has no responsibility. [...] God's sovereignty in salvation [however] is because God is the creator of man, and, like a potter, He can make the vessel for whatever purpose He has for the vessel.

[...] Many people question the basis of God's election. If God does elect some for mercy, then how does He choose? Some say it must be based on the works of men, but verse 11, along with many other passages, clearly states that it is not of works (Ephesians 2:8-9; Titus 3:5). Others will state that, if God's election is not based on man's works, then it must be that God's choice is based on man's choice for God. However, that is not what this passage states. This passage clearly states that God does the choosing—not based on anything that man has done.

So what is the basis of God's election? It is simply this: God's election is based on God's glory and God's glory alone. The purpose of God's election is to display His mercy. Salvation is for God to show His mercy. It is not for man. It is not about man—it is about God!

If God sent all men to Hell, there would be no display of His mercy. Therefore, He has shown mercy on whom He wills. It is because God, as the Sovereign of the universe, has the right and the authority to elect some to mercy. There is no way to understand God's election to mercy unless we understand God's sovereignty. That is the basis of Paul's whole argument. God is sovereign and can do whatever He wills and does not have to answer to man, angels, or anything else for His decisions. [...] The reason this issue is so difficult to understand is because people think that only one action can cause a single reaction. In other words, [they think that] either God chooses or man chooses—that it cannot be both.

[...] Most Christians would agree on the doctrine of inspiration. This doctrine teaches that God used men to write the Bible, that men like Paul, used their own words not dictated by God. However, we call it the Word of God and rightfully so. For it is God's Word in every sense. Paul wrote Romans, yet God superintended each letter so that every word, in its original writing, was without error or flaw. Superintended means that the inscripturation of God's Word was by the control and guidance of the Holy Spirit (2 Peter 1:20-21). It was supernatural. It was a heightening of man's abilities and sensibilities.

The result was that God wrote the book of Romans, and we can also say that Paul wrote the book of Romans. Both are the single author of the book of Romans. Most Christians agree with this statement when it comes to the doctrine of inspiration. So let us summarize it: God worked through men to write in their words to create the Bible, yet the Holy Spirit controlled every letter so that it was written exactly as God intended it to be written.

The doctrine of inspiration teaches us that God works through people so that the choices they make are God's choices. [...] So, God works through people to make the choices that He desires, but it is still man's responsibility for his choices.

Now, let us carry that over to the doctrine of salvation and the discussion of the sovereignty of God and the responsibility of man. There is a good reason why God places Romans chapter 10 after Romans chapter 9. That was to prevent much of the debate that too many Christians spend their time arguing over.

You see the struggle over this doctrine is a struggle over our theological understanding and our experience. We have just seen that theologically it is God, and God alone, who elects to show mercy on whomever He chooses. However, when we got saved, what did we experience? We remember someone presenting the gospel to us and we believed. Therefore, experientially we remember our choosing God. Therefore, the debate around who chose whom is really an issue of our theological understanding versus our experience. However, they do not have to be mutually exclusive. One does not have to happen before the other. Therefore, did God choose you or did you choose God?

Regeneration

Regeneration is a supernatural work of the Holy Spirit by which a new nature and eternal life are given. It is the new life implanted in the heart of a believer and is the restoration of the original God given tendencies toward God before the fall. After the fall, man's will is to sin; after regeneration, man's will is to glorify God because of the indwelling Holy Spirit:

> Jesus answered him, "Truly, truly, I say to you, unless one is born again he cannot see the kingdom of God." Nicodemus said to him, "How can a man be born when he is old? Can he enter a second time into his mother's womb and be born?" Jesus answered, "Truly, truly, I say to you, unless one is born of water and the Spirit, he cannot enter the kingdom of God. That which is born of the flesh is flesh, and that which is born of the Spirit is spirit. Do not marvel that I said to you, 'You must be born again' (John 3:3–7).

Therefore, if anyone is in Christ, he is a new creation. The old has passed away; behold, the new has come. All this is from God, who through Christ reconciled us to himself and gave us the ministry of reconciliation (2 Corinthians 5:17–18).

He saved us, not because of works done by us in righteousness, but according to his own mercy, by the washing of regeneration and renewal of the Holy Spirit (Titus 3:5).

Regeneration is instantaneous and is accomplished solely by the power of the Holy Spirit through the instrumentality of the Word of God (John 5:24) when the repentant sinner, as enabled by the Holy Spirit, responds in faith to the divine provision of salvation. Regeneration is not based on any works of man, nor is it assisted by man's works.

Genuine regeneration is manifested by fruits worthy of repentance as demonstrated in righteous attitudes and conduct. Good works will be its proper evidence and fruit and will be experienced to the extent that the believer submits to the control of the Holy Spirit in his life through faithful obedience to the Word of God. This is called the filling of the Holy Spirit:

For we are his workmanship, created in Christ Jesus for good works, which God prepared beforehand, that we should walk in them (Ephesians 2:10).

What good is it, my brothers, if someone says he has faith but does not have works? Can that faith save him? If a brother or sister is poorly clothed and lacking in daily food, and one of you says to them, "Go in peace, be warmed and filled," without giving them the things needed for the body, what good is that? So also faith by itself, if it does not have works, is dead.

But someone will say, "You have faith and I have works." Show me your faith apart from your works, and I will show you my faith by my works. You believe that God is one; you do well. Even the demons believe—and shudder! Do you want to be shown, you foolish person, that faith apart from works is useless? Was not Abraham our father justified by works when he offered up his son Isaac on the altar? You see that faith was active along with his works, and faith was completed by his works; and the Scripture was fulfilled that says, "Abraham believed God, and it was counted to him as righteousness"—and he was called a friend of God. You see that a person is justified by works and not by faith alone. And in the same way was not also Rahab the prostitute justified by works when she received the messengers and sent them out by another way? (James 2:14–25).

Therefore do not be foolish, but understand what the will of the Lord is. And do not get drunk with wine, for that is debauchery, but be filled with the Spirit, addressing one another in psalms and hymns and spiritual songs, singing and making melody to the Lord with your heart, giving thanks always and for everything to God the Father in the name of our

Lord Jesus Christ, submitting to one another out of reverence for Christ (Ephesians 5:17–21).

This obedience causes the believer to be increasingly conformed to the image of our Lord Jesus Christ, *"And we all, with unveiled face, beholding the glory of the Lord, are being transformed into the same image from one degree of glory to another. For this comes from the Lord who is the Spirit"* (2 Corinthians 3:18). Scripture shows us that this conformity climaxes in the believer's glorification at Christ's coming:

> *And if children, then heirs—heirs of God and fellow heirs with Christ, provided we suffer with him in order that we may also be glorified with him* (Romans 8:17).

> *His divine power has granted to us all things that pertain to life and godliness, through the knowledge of him who called us to his own glory and excellence, by which he has granted to us his precious and very great promises, so that through them you may become partakers of the divine nature, having escaped from the corruption that is in the world because of sinful desire* (2 Peter 1:4).

> *Beloved, we are God's children now, and what we will be has not yet appeared; but we know that when he appears we shall be like him, because we shall see him as he is. And everyone who thus hopes in him purifies himself as he is pure* (1 John 3:2–3).

Conversion

Conversion is man's voluntary turning from sin to God. Conversion is a twofold turning, first from sin and second to God. Conversion is man's confession and belief. There are two characteristics that describe conversion: repentance and faith. See the following verses from Romans:

> *Because, if you confess with your mouth that Jesus is Lord and believe in your heart that God raised him from the dead, you will be saved. For with the heart one believes and is justified, and with the mouth one confesses and is saved* (Romans 10:9–10).

Repentance

Repentance is intellectually, emotionally, and voluntary turning from sin. The turning to God must also involve all three, because that is the entire makeup of man, and, at the fall, man became corrupt intellectually, emotionally, and voluntary. This is usually the cause of contention with some, in that, they believe man cannot repent until these three parts of man are regenerated. However, due to the reality that regeneration and repentance occur simultaneously, the intellect, emotion, and will are regenerated at the same point of repentance.

Many people can intellectually understand a need to turn from sin. Some even have the capacity to be emotional about it. But only those whose volition (will) is changed (regeneration) experience salvation. It is because our will is depraved that it is not free from the control of sin until conversion. Repentance is God's desire for all men:

The times of ignorance God overlooked, but now he commands all people everywhere to repent (Acts 17:30).

The Lord is not slow to fulfill his promise as some count slowness, but is patient toward you, not wishing that any should perish, but that all should reach repentance (2 Peter 3:9).

Faith

Faith is intellectually, emotionally, and voluntary turning to God. Some would believe that faith is capable within the nature of man—that man has the capacity to turn to God. This stems from a false view of the effects of the fall of man. Man cannot, within himself, turn to God intellectually, emotionally, and voluntary.

Many people can intellectually understand a need to turn to God and the gospel. Some even have the capacity to be emotional about it. But, once again, only those whose volition (will) is changed (regeneration) experience salvation. Many people, such as Pelagius, struggle with the concept of total depravity because man is able to understand the Gospel of God at least intellectually and/or emotionally, and, therefore, they assume that man is capable of volitionally turning to God.

The following are more excerpts from the message titled "God's Sovereignty and Human Responsibility in Salvation":

Romans 10:9-10 clearly states that if we confess and believe, we will be saved. The basis of our salvation was our confession and belief. It does not matter if you are a Jew or Gentile. Anyone who confesses with their mouth the Lord Jesus Christ and believes in their heart that God raised Him from the dead will be saved.

[...] We can come up with many, many arguments, but this text is very clear: *"whosoever calls upon the name of the Lord shall be saved."*

Now let us deal with one of the major arguments against this text. It is the view that man cannot believe in God until God regenerates the man and changes his heart to be able to believe in God. Not only does this passage teach against that view, but it also leads to one of two dangerous teachings that many do not realize. If God must regenerate a person to be able to believe then you have put a time gap between regeneration and belief. You now have the problem that, if someone is not saved until they believe and that person must be regenerated first, then they can be regenerated and yet not be saved. Thus, you can be a regenerated unbeliever, and this cannot happen—even if it is for a split second. No one can be a regenerated unbeliever. However, if you err on the other side of man choosing God, now you have an unregenerate believer. Again, you have the same problem.

So what is the answer? Well, let us go back to what we said about the doctrine of inspiration. We have already seen that the Holy Spirit works through men to do what God wills, though it is completely by their own willful acts. Note, I did not say free will, because no one prior to salvation has a free will. We are all influenced by sin; therefore, until salvation our will is not free. It is bound by sin.

[...] Therefore, when we discuss the doctrine of God's sovereignty in salvation, we see that man does have a responsibility, and yet it is God's election. Regeneration and man's belief are a simultaneous work of the Holy Spirit. One does not happen without the other. God elected outside of time and worked through us, by convicting us of our sin, so that we would confess and believe.

Now, for those who are still confused and are convinced that they must be able to understand these two elements of salvation completely, there is one more Scripture that will completely answer this debate. It is Deuteronomy 29:29. It says, "*The secret things belong to the Lord our God, but those things which are revealed belong to us and to our children forever, that we may do all the words of this law.*"

In other words, it is not for us to know everything about God, but, that which He has revealed to us, we have a responsibility to teach others. God is greater than we are, and His ways are not our ways; therefore, we are not expected to understand everything of God. If you cannot fully comprehend how God can elect us apart from our choosing and yet we choose God, then that is fine. You do not have to understand it fully; know that

God has taught it, and teach it as He has revealed it
to us through Paul.

Justification

Justification before God is an act of God (Romans 8:33)
by which He legally declares righteous those who, through
faith in Christ alone, repent of their sins (Luke 13:3; Acts
2:38; 3:19; 11:18; Romans 2:4; 2 Corinthians 7:10; Isaiah
55:6-7) and confess Him as sovereign Lord (Romans 10:9-
10; 1 Corinthians 12:3; 2 Corinthians 4:5; Philippians 2:11).

Justification is being declared just and no longer
condemned; it is the declaring of one as righteous.
Justification does not change one's spiritual condition and
make one righteous in and of himself (i.e., perfectly holy in
the present age). This righteousness is apart from any virtue
or work of man: *"For by works of the law no human being
will be justified in his sight, since through the law comes
knowledge of sin"* (Romans 3:20). It also involves the
imputation of our sins to Christ (Colossians 2:14; 1 Peter
2:24) and the imputation of Christ's righteousness to us (1
Corinthians 1:30; 2 Corinthians 5:21). By this, we mean that
God is enabled to *"be just and the justifier of the one who
has faith in Jesus"* (Romans 3:26). Only God, as judge, can
declare one as just.

Sanctification

Sanctification is the growth of the implanted new
nature (it follows regeneration). It is natural for all things to
grow after they are born. The same is true in the spiritual
realm. This is a continuing consequence of union with
Christ. Therefore, there is a logical and chronological order

to sanctification, which occurs only after regeneration. Something must be born before it can grow.

Every believer is sanctified (set apart) unto God by justification and is declared to be holy, being identified as a saint. Being sanctified is positional and instantaneous and should not be confused with progressive sanctification, which is the process after regeneration until death or glorification. Being sanctified has to do with the believer's standing, not his present walk or condition. See the following passages:

> And now I commend you to God and to the word of his grace, which is able to build you up and to give you the inheritance among all those who are sanctified (Acts 20:32).

> To the church of God that is in Corinth, to those sanctified in Christ Jesus, called to be saints together with all those who in every place call upon the name of our Lord Jesus Christ, both their Lord and ours (1 Corinthians 1:2).

> And because of him you are in Christ Jesus, who became to us wisdom from God, righteousness and sanctification and redemption (1 Corinthians 1:30).

> And such were some of you. But you were washed, you were sanctified, you were justified in the name of the Lord Jesus Christ and by the Spirit of our God (1 Corinthians 6:11).

> But we ought always to give thanks to God for you, brothers beloved by the Lord, because God chose

you as the firstfruits to be saved, through sanctification by the Spirit and belief in the truth (2 Thessalonians 2:13).

For he who sanctifies and those who are sanctified all have one source. That is why he is not ashamed to call them brothers (Hebrews 2:11).

Therefore, holy brothers, you who share in a heavenly calling, consider Jesus, the apostle and high priest of our confession (Hebrews 3:1).

And by that will we have been sanctified through the offering of the body of Jesus Christ once for all (Hebrews 10:10).

For by a single offering he has perfected for all time those who are being sanctified (Hebrews 10:14).

So Jesus also suffered outside the gate in order to sanctify the people through his own blood (Hebrews 13:12).

[...] according to the foreknowledge of God the Father, in the sanctification of the Spirit, for obedience to Jesus Christ and for sprinkling with his blood: May grace and peace be multiplied to you (1 Peter 1:2).

There is also, by the work of the Holy Spirit, a progressive sanctification by which the state of the believer is brought closer to the standing that the believer positionally enjoys through justification. Through obedience to the Word of God and the empowering of the Holy Spirit, the believer is able to live a life of increasing holiness in conformity to the will of God, becoming more and more like our Lord Jesus Christ. This process is never complete until the death of the body. See the following Scriptures:

Sanctify them in the truth; your word is truth (John 17:17).

And for their sake I consecrate myself, that they also may be sanctified in truth (John 17:19).

What shall we say then? Are we to continue in sin that grace may abound? By no means! How can we who died to sin still live in it? Do you not know that all of us who have been baptized into Christ Jesus were baptized into his death? We were buried therefore with him by baptism into death, in order that, just as Christ was raised from the dead by the glory of the Father, we too might walk in newness of life.

For if we have been united with him in a death like his, we shall certainly be united with him in a resurrection like his. We know that our old self was crucified with him in order that the body of sin might be brought to nothing, so that we would no longer be enslaved to sin. For one who has died has been set free from sin. Now if we have died with Christ, we believe that we will also live with him. We know that Christ, being raised from the dead, will never die again; death no longer has dominion over him. For the death he died he died to sin, once for all, but the life he lives he lives to God. So you also must consider yourselves dead to sin and alive to God in Christ Jesus.

Let not sin therefore reign in your mortal body, to make you obey its passions. Do not present your members to sin as instruments for unrighteousness, but present yourselves to God as those who have been brought from death to life, and your members to God as instruments for righteousness. For sin will have no dominion over you, since you are not under law but under grace.

What then? Are we to sin because we are not under law but under grace? By no means! Do you not know that if you present yourselves to anyone as obedient slaves, you are slaves of the one whom you obey, either of sin, which leads to death, or of obedience, which leads to righteousness? But thanks be to God, that you who were once slaves of sin have become obedient from the heart to the standard of teaching to which you were committed, and, having been set free from sin, have become slaves of righteousness. I am speaking in human terms, because of your natural limitations. For just as you once presented your members as slaves to impurity and to lawlessness leading to more lawlessness, so now present your members as slaves to righteousness leading to sanctification.

For when you were slaves of sin, you were free in regard to righteousness. But what fruit were you getting at that time from the things of which you are now ashamed? For the end of those things is death.

But now that you have been set free from sin and have become slaves of God, the fruit you get leads to sanctification and its end, eternal life (Romans 6:1–22).

And we all, with unveiled face, beholding the glory of the Lord, are being transformed into the same image from one degree of glory to another. For this comes from the Lord who is the Spirit (2 Corinthians 3:18).

For this is the will of God, your sanctification: that you abstain from sexual immorality; that each one of you know how to control his own body in holiness and honor (1 Thessalonians 4:3–4).

Now may the God of peace himself sanctify you completely, and may your whole spirit and soul and body be kept blameless at the coming of our Lord Jesus Christ (1 Thessalonians 5:23).

In this respect, every saved person is involved in a daily conflict. The new creation in Christ is doing battle against the flesh, but adequate provision is made for victory through the power of the indwelling Holy Spirit. This struggle, nevertheless, stays with the believer all through this earthly life and is never completely ended until eternity. All claims to the eradication of sin in this life are unscriptural. Eradication of sin in this life is not possible, but the Holy Spirit does provide for victory over sin:

But I say, walk by the Spirit, and you will not gratify the desires of the flesh. For the desires of the flesh are against the Spirit, and the desires of the Spirit are against the flesh, for these are opposed to each other, to keep you from doing the things you want to do. But if you are led by the Spirit, you are not under the law. Now the works of the flesh are evident: sexual immorality, impurity, sensuality, idolatry, sorcery, enmity, strife, jealousy, fits of anger, rivalries, dissensions, divisions, envy, drunkenness, orgies, and things like these. I warn you, as I warned you before, that those who do such things will not inherit the kingdom of God. But the fruit of the Spirit is love, joy, peace, patience, kindness, goodness, faithfulness, gentleness, self-control; against such things there is no law. And those who belong to Christ Jesus have crucified the flesh with its passions and desires. If we live by the Spirit, let us also keep in step with the Spirit (Galatians 5:16–25).

[...] to put off your old self, which belongs to your former manner of life and is corrupt through deceitful desires, and to be renewed in the spirit of your minds, and to put on the new self, created after the likeness of God in true righteousness and holiness (Ephesians 4:22–24).

Not that I have already obtained this or am already perfect, but I press on to make it my own, because Christ Jesus has made me his own (Philippians 3:12).

Do not lie to one another, seeing that you have put off the old self with its practices and have put on the new self, which is being renewed in knowledge after the image of its creator (Colossians 3:9–10).

As obedient children, do not be conformed to the passions of your former ignorance, but as he who called you is holy, you also be holy in all your conduct, since it is written, "You shall be holy, for I am holy" (1 Peter 1:14–16).

You know that he appeared in order to take away sins, and in him there is no sin. No one who abides in him keeps on sinning; no one who keeps on sinning has either seen him or known him. Little children, let no one deceive you. Whoever practices righteousness is righteous, as he is righteous. Whoever makes a practice of sinning is of the devil, for the devil has been sinning from the beginning. The reason the Son of God appeared was to destroy the works of the devil. No one born of God makes a practice of sinning, for God's seed abides in him; and he cannot keep on sinning, because he has been born of God (1 John 3:5–9).

Separation from sin is clearly mandated throughout the Old and New Testaments, and the Scriptures clearly indicate that in the last days apostasy and worldliness shall increase:

Do not be unequally yoked with unbelievers. For what partnership has righteousness with lawlessness? Or what fellowship has light with darkness? What accord has Christ with Belial? Or what portion does a believer share with an unbeliever? What agreement has the temple of God with idols? For we are the temple of the living God; as God said, "I will make my dwelling among them and walk among them, and I will be their God, and they shall be my people. Therefore go out from their midst, and be separate from them, says the Lord, and touch no unclean thing; then I will welcome you, and I will be a father to you, and you shall be sons and daughters to me, says the Lord Almighty." Since we have these promises, beloved, let us cleanse ourselves from every defilement of body and spirit, bringing holiness to completion in the fear of God (2 Corinthians 6:14–7:1).

But understand this, that in the last days there will come times of difficulty. For people will be lovers of self, lovers of money, proud, arrogant, abusive, disobedient to their parents, ungrateful, unholy, heartless, unappeasable, slanderous, without self-control, brutal, not loving good, treacherous, reckless, swollen with conceit, lovers of pleasure rather than lovers of God, having the appearance of godliness, but denying its power. Avoid such people (2 Timothy 3:1–5).

Out of deep gratitude for the undeserved grace of God granted to us and because our glorious God is so worthy of our total consecration, all believers should live in such a manner as to demonstrate their adoring love to God so as not to bring reproach upon our Lord and Savior. God commands us, as His children, to be separate from all religious apostasy and worldly, sinful practices:

I appeal to you therefore, brothers, by the mercies of God, to present your bodies as a living sacrifice, holy and acceptable to God, which is your spiritual worship. Do not be conformed to this world, but be transformed by the renewal of your mind, that by testing you may discern what is the will of God, what is good and acceptable and perfect (Romans 12:1–2).

I wrote to you in my letter not to associate with sexually immoral people—not at all meaning the sexually immoral of this world, or the greedy and swindlers, or idolaters, since then you would need to go out of the world. But now I am writing to you not to associate with anyone who bears the name of brother if he is guilty of sexual immorality or greed, or is an idolater, reviler, drunkard, or swindler—not even to eat with such a one. For what have I to do with judging outsiders? Is it not those inside the church whom you are to judge? God judges those outside. "Purge the evil person from among you" (1 Corinthians 5:9–13).

Do not love the world or the things in the world. If anyone loves the world, the love of the Father is not in him. 16 For all that is in the world—the desires of the flesh and the desires of the eyes and pride of life[a]—is not from the Father but is from the world. 17 And the world is passing away along with its desires, but whoever does the will of God abides forever (1 John 2:15–17).

Everyone who goes on ahead and does not abide in the teaching of Christ, does not have God. Whoever abides in the teaching has both the Father and the Son. If anyone comes to you and does not bring this

teaching, do not receive him into your house or give
him any greeting, for whoever greets him takes part
in his wicked works (2 John 9–11).

Believers should be separated unto the Lord Jesus Christ
(2 Thessalonians 1:11-12; Hebrews 12:1-2) and affirm that
the Christian life is a life of obedient righteousness that
reflects the teaching of the Beatitudes (Matthew 5:2-12)
and a continual pursuit of holiness (Romans 12:1-2; 2
Corinthians 7:1; Hebrews 12:14; Titus 2:11-14; 1 John 3:1-
10).

Perseverance

Perseverance is voluntarily continuing in the faith. It is
the human side of sanctification and can only occur after
regeneration. While sanctification measures the degree of
maturity, perseverance measures the degree of yielding,
and assurance measures the degree of confidence.

It is the privilege of believers to rejoice in the assurance
of their salvation through the testimony of God's Word.
Scripture, however, clearly forbids the use of Christian
liberty and assurance as an occasion for sinful living and
carnality (Romans 6:15-22; 13:13-14; Galatians 5:13, 25-26;
Titus 2:11-14). All of the redeemed are kept by God's power
and are thus eternally secure in Christ forever, and they will
persevere:

"Truly, truly, I say to you, whoever hears my word
and believes him who sent me has eternal life. He
does not come into judgment, but has passed from
death to life" (John 5:24).

"All that the Father gives me will come to me, and whoever comes to me I will never cast out. For I have come down from heaven, not to do my own will but the will of him who sent me. And this is the will of him who sent me, that I should lose nothing of all that he has given me, but raise it up on the last day. For this is the will of my Father, that everyone who looks on the Son and believes in him should have eternal life, and I will raise him up on the last day" (John 6:37–40).

"My sheep hear my voice, and I know them, and they follow me. I give them eternal life, and they will never perish, and no one will snatch them out of my hand. My Father, who has given them to me, is greater than all, and no one is able to snatch them out of the Father's hand. I and the Father are one" (John 10:27–30).

Since, therefore, we have now been justified by his blood, much more shall we be saved by him from the wrath of God. For if while we were enemies we were reconciled to God by the death of his Son, much more, now that we are reconciled, shall we be saved by his life (Romans 5:9–10).

There is therefore now no condemnation for those who are in Christ Jesus. For the law of the Spirit of life has set you free in Christ Jesus from the law of sin and death (Romans 8:1-2).

What then shall we say to these things? If God is for us, who can be against us? He who did not spare his own Son but gave him up for us all, how will he not also with him graciously give us all things? Who shall bring any charge against God's elect? It is God who justifies. Who is to condemn? Christ Jesus is the one who died—more than that, who was raised—who is at the right hand of God, who indeed is interceding for us. Who shall separate us from the love of Christ? Shall tribulation, or distress, or persecution, or famine, or nakedness, or danger, or sword? As it is written, "For your sake we are being killed all the day long; we are regarded as sheep to be slaughtered." No, in all these things we are more than conquerors through him who loved us. For I am sure that neither death nor life, nor angels nor rulers, nor things present nor things to come, nor powers, nor height nor depth, nor anything else in all creation, will be able to separate us from the love of God in Christ Jesus our Lord (Romans 8:31–39).

I give thanks to my God always for you because of the grace of God that was given you in Christ Jesus, that in every way you were enriched in him in all speech and all knowledge—even as the testimony about Christ was confirmed among you—so that you are not lacking in any gift, as you wait for the revealing of our Lord Jesus Christ, who will sustain you to the end, guiltless in the day of our Lord Jesus Christ (1 Corinthians 1:4–8).

And do not grieve the Holy Spirit of God, by whom you were sealed for the day of redemption (Ephesians 4:30).

Consequently, he is able to save to the uttermost those who draw near to God through him, since he always lives to make intercession for them (Hebrews 7:25).

Keep your life free from love of money, and be content with what you have, for he has said, "I will never leave you nor forsake you" (Hebrews 13:5).

[...] who by God's power are being guarded through faith for a salvation ready to be revealed in the last time (1 Peter 1:5).

Now to him who is able to keep you from stumbling and to present you blameless before the presence of his glory with great joy, to the only God, our Savior, through Jesus Christ our Lord, be glory, majesty, dominion, and authority, before all time and now and forever. Amen (Jude 24-25).

Chapter 8

The Church

We believe that the church is made of regenerate people who meet for the worship of God and are called the body of Christ.

Definition

The term "the church" brings up many different ideas for different people. Some think of the church as a building where people meet to worship God. Some think of it as a particular Christian organization, typically one with its own clergy, buildings, and distinctive doctrines (e.g. the Church of England). Others think of it as the hierarchy of clergy within a Christian organization (especially within the Roman Catholic Church.) Some define it as institutionalized religion acting as a political or social force. Some refer to it as the people of God. Which is the correct definition when there is such a variety of meaning? And, within Christian doctrine, what specifically is "the church"?

ἐκκλησία (ekklēsía)

The term most often translated "church" is ἐκκλησία (ekklēsía) in the Greek. This term has the meaning of an assembly or congregation and appears over 100 times in the New Testament. The Greek translation of the Hebrew Old Testament, called the Septuagint, most often translates ἐκκλησία as קָהָל (qā·hāl). קָהָל is used over 57 times of the

97 uses of *ἐκκλησία* in the Old Testament (Septuagint) and refers to an assembly, congregation, army, or crowd.

ἐκκλησία had several meanings in the first century[10:]

1) a regularly summoned legislative body or assembly
2) a casual gathering of people or an assemblage
3) people with shared belief, community, or congregation

The first meaning was a generally understood concept in the Greco-Roman world, and, in Ephesus, this was even used for the theater. The last meaning is the one that was used often in the Old and New Testament.

The root word of *ἐκκλησία* means to "call out" or be "called out." It was a common term for a congregation of the *ekklētoí*, the called people, or those called out or assembled in the public affairs of a free state, the body of free citizens called together by a herald (*kérux*) which constituted the *ekklēsía*. [...] The word *ekklēsía* is nowhere used of heathen religious assemblies in Scripture.[11]

In regards to the biblical history of the word *ἐκκλησία*, it originally meant any public assembly of citizens summoned by a herald.[12]

The Historical Meaning

The term *ἐκκλησία* was not specifically a Christian term, but, over time, *ἐκκλησία* came to have a more specific reference to a more specific assembly or congregation that we call "the church." Thus, in the Greek world, it was used for a public assembly summoned by a herald.[13] By indicating that the use of the term changed, we are referring to the change in use from the wider and secular Greco-Roman use of the word to the biblical use of the word. This constitutes what might best be called a narrowing of the definition of the word from a general sense of assemblage to a particular sense of assemblage around certain doctrines and parameters.

The following quote from John Calvin addresses an issue that has been the cause of tension in defining the church and the interpretation of the Bible for 2,000 years. This issue is the continuity and discontinuity of the congregation of Israel and the church:

> From an early period it has been recognized that, while the church is one and catholic [unified], it presents different aspects or forms which call for differentiation in reference. Thus already in the Bible itself there is distinction between the OT church and the NT church. It would be wrong to deduce from this a complete dichotomy, as though the NT church were something quite different which began only at some point in the NT story, e.g., at Pentecost. On the other hand, it would be pointless to deny that there are valid differences between the OT church and the NT church. A legitimate distinction may thus be drawn.[14]

A covenantal point of view would stress that there is basic substantial continuity and administrative discontinuity between the church before Pentecost and the church after Pentecost. Alternatively, the dispensational point of view would stress a discontinuity and see separation between Old Testament Israel and the New Testament church.

Though there is this difference about the makeup of the Old Testament congregation and how they relate to the New Testament church, both sides agree that the church has a specific meaning in the current age. The point, on which both theological systems agree as regards their main theme, is that you cannot biblically get away with defining the church as just any old group of people who got together for any old purpose or reason.

The covenantal view would stress that there is substantial continuity between the old covenant church and the new covenant church. That is to say, the substance—the thing that makes it what it is—is the same in both the old and new covenants. Nevertheless, as already stated, there is a fundamental discontinuity of administration, i.e., the ordinances and rules of the organization.

In the covenantal view, the old covenant particularly associated with Moses and Mt. Sinai was a covenant of types and shadows which pointed to Christ. These types and shadows were to instruct those under that administration to look to Christ in faith, just as the reality is to perform the same purpose in the new covenant. The Passover lamb was a picture of Christ and was meant to teach the people whom God had chosen for himself and to save them from death and judgment.

From the same substance, there is a different administration. We no longer have animal sacrifice. This is because under the new covenant we do not need shadows to point us to Christ. We have the reality. Praise God for the reality of the cross and resurrection!

In any case, the point of this discussion is that you cannot say, as a covenantalist, that the church has ever been just any old group of people. God has always defined what the church is and who is a member of the church. From the time of Adam to the time of Abraham, it was those whom God called to himself out of darkness into the light. Often few in number and greatly persecuted, they were still called out by God. From the time of Abraham to the time of Moses, God particularly dealt with Abraham's descendants and commanded them to take the sign of circumcision. From the time of Moses to the time of Christ, God gave the strictest outward rules in all of redemptive history regarding who could be a member of his covenant people.

Dispensationists, though, do not have the problem of trying to separate an Old Testament church and the New Testament church because dispensationalism already sees and assumes a separation between the two. They do not see Israel as the church, even though there was a congregation known as Israel that would meet at the temple or the local synagogue and would closely resemble the New Testament congregation known as the church.

What is important to note between these two viewpoints is that even those who see Israel as the Old Testament church see the church as a specific entity. Still, as we will see, the idea of the church or general gathering of a congregation transitioned after Pentecost into a specific group of people who practice specific functions.

Early Church

When Paul spoke of the church, he did so without thought of separate congregations, but as one church. Though Paul wrote to individual groups of congregations that were recognized as separate and distinct, he also saw the true believers as one church. As the congregations of believers met for the purpose of the worship of God, the term church started to have a more specific meaning, denoting a specific group of people who function in a specific manner.

Thus, the word ἐκκλησία took on a new and more specifically Christian meaning. It no longer referred to a general gathering or assembly of people, but to a group that meets for the worship of God, the reading and explaining of His Word, and the practicing of the ordinances (baptism and communion). It also referred to the purity of the group, i.e., church discipline, but, we must note that the early church did not seem to make much of a distinction between different local congregations.

Church of the Middle Ages

As the church moved into the Middle Ages, theologians started to be more specific about the meaning of the church by making a distinction between what they called the "visible church" and the "invisible church," or the local and universal church respectively. This distinction was made to refer to the body of all believers in Jesus Christ (invisible church), and those local congregations who met for the worship of God but could have unbelievers in their midst (visible church).

The invisible or universal church is the body of believers everywhere in the world throughout time. The universal church is made up of only and all believers. When people speak of the church as a group of people who believe in God and who have repented, this is a reference to the church. When a person is converted to Jesus Christ they are immediately made a member of this universal church. It is called the "invisible church" because we, as human beings, cannot see who is and who is not a participant of the church. In other words, we cannot see who are believers and who are non-believers.

The second distinction is the local or visible church. This reference to the church is the local gathering of people for the purpose of fulfilling the function of the church. However, unlike the universal church, this reference to the church can refer to a group of people, but this group of people is not exclusively made up of converted believers in Jesus Christ. The local church refers to a local congregation of people, believers and non-believers, who gather regularly for the purpose of the worship of God. In a time when church attendance was almost mandatory or expected, there were many who would gather in the local church who could not truly worship God and fulfill the function of the church because they were not believers.

Therefore, the Middle Ages provided us with two more specific definitions of the term "the church." These definitions help us distinguish between the world-wide group of those who truly believe and local gatherings which can contain true and false converts to Christ.

The Reformation Church

During the Reformation, the examination of the definition of the church received much attention. After the helpful definitions from the Middle Ages of the universal and local church, the focus became about the function of the local church. During the Reformation, the Puritans' definition of the church was based on three functions of the church:

1) The proclamation of the Word of God,
2) The practice of the ordinances (i.e., baptism and communion), and
3) The keeping of the purity of the church through church discipline.

These three functions become the definition of the local church in purpose. The Puritans would say that if a local church were not practicing all three of these elements, then they were not a church. Therefore, we see that "the church" was further defined through questioning the role of the church and reforming the Roman Catholic Church.

As we see throughout history, the base definition of the church as "a gathering of people" continued to become more and more specific in nature. In time, the definition went from "a general gathering" to "a gathering of believers for the purpose of the worship of God"; then, to distinguish between all those who are truly believers in Christ ("the universal church") and to those who gather for worship regularly ("the local church"); and, finally, the definition was based upon local church function.

Under the overarching rule of the Roman Catholic Church, which defined the church as an organization that could determine the salvation of individuals and declared themselves as the only arbiters of the Scripture, the reformers responded with a major emphasis on the definition of the church and how much authority it should have over individuals. They did not disagree with the early church's definitions but added more specifics. Calvin states:

"The form of the true church appears and stands forth conspicuous to our view. Wherever we see the word of God sincerely preached and heard, wherever we see the sacraments administered according to the institution of Christ, there we cannot have any doubt that the church of God has some existence, since his promise cannot fail, "Where two or three are gathered together in my name, there am I in the midst of them" (Matth. xviii. 20). But that we may have a clear summary of this subject, we must proceed by the following steps:-- The Church universal is the multitude collected out of all nations, who, though dispersed and far distant from each other, agree in one truth of divine doctrine, and are bound together by the tie of a common religion. In this way it comprehends single churches, which exist in different towns and villages, according to the wants of human society, so that each of them justly obtains the name and authority of the Church; and also comprehends single individuals, who by a religious profession are accounted to belong to such churches, although they are in fact aliens from the Church, but have not been cut off by a public decision.[15]

As we can see from Calvin, the church was then defined as the local believers who gather for the purpose of the worship of God through the proclamation of the Scriptures, the practice of the ordinances, and keeping the purity through church discipline. Thus, the meaning of "the church" continued to be more and more refined.

Modern Church

In the recent age, with the rise of Dispensationalism, the definition of the church had, once again, been further clarified and specified. An evaluation of the long-held Roman Catholic teaching of Israel as the Old Testament church was being rethought. Dispensationalism made a differentiation between Old Testament Israel and the New Testament church. They saw a discontinuity between Israel and the church.

According to this thought, Israel is not the church and the church is not Israel. This does not change the previous definitions of the church and would agree with the covenant definition of the church; but it limits the definition to the New Testament church and does not trace this definition back into Old Testament Israel. This distinction helps to further clarify the definition of the church developed so far throughout history, but it applies this definition only to those believers after Pentecost, locally gathering for the function of the church.

Throughout history, we see the progression of the definition of "the church" move from a general term referring to any gathering of people to a very specific definition referring to a special group of people, the function of those people, and, finally, also the time period in which they lived.

Conclusion

So we see that the definition of the church continues to be refined into a more and more specific meaning. Therefore, when some say that the church is any group of believers, they are right but not specific enough anymore. As theologians continued to address issues throughout church history, they had to continue being more specific in their definition of "the church."

It should be noted that some use Matthew 18:20 to explain what makes up the church: *"For where two or three are gathered in my name, there am I among them."* The purpose of this passage, however, is to address church discipline; it is not a passage that is about defining the church. Nevertheless, it does affect the definition of the church by discussing its function, which the reformers added to the definition. Arguing that the church is limited to any gathering of two or three believers ignores the context of Matthew 18, which presents the idea of church discipline as a vital part of church function.

Clearly, to have a gathering of people requires more than just one person. But does any gathering of believers make a church? If this definition is true, then any two believers that work together would be a church. After evaluating the definition through Scripture and history, we see that the church is where people gather for the function of the church. Some have argued that when Christians go out onto the streets to evangelize, that is defined as church. Wayne Grudem makes a case against this view:

> Baptism and the Lord's Supper also serve as "membership controls" for the church. Baptism is the means for admitting people into the church, and the Lord's Supper is the means for allowing people to give a sign of continuing in the membership of the church—the church signifies that it considers those who receive baptism and the Lord's Supper to be saved. Therefore, these activities indicate what a church thinks about salvation, and they are appropriately listed as a mark of the church today as well. By contrast, groups who do not administer baptism and the Lord's Supper signify that they are not intending to function as a church. Someone may stand on a street corner with a small crowd and have true preaching and hearing of the Word, but the people there would not be a church. Even a neighborhood Bible study meeting in a home can have the true teaching and hearing of the Word without becoming a church. But if a local Bible study began baptizing its own new converts and regularly participating in the Lord's Supper, these things would signify an intention to function as a church, and it would be difficult to say why it should not be considered a church in itself.[16]

In conclusion, we can see throughout history that the church is a local gathering of people for the functioning of the proclamation of God's Word, practicing of the ordinance, and concern for purity by church discipline. As believers, it is expected that we should be actively part of the church, serving others through the spiritual gifts that the Holy Spirit gave to us at salvation.

Chapter 9

The Eternal State

We believe in a literal heaven and hell that will be conscious and permanent.

The eternal state is the conscious state in which man will live, both body and soul, for all eternity. The aspects that Christians need to address are death, the intermediate state, and the final eternal state. There is much confusion on these subjects.

Death

The concept of death is separation. Death is the result of sin. There are three types of death: physical, spiritual, and eternal. Physical death is the separation of the spirit from the body. The spirit does NOT cease to exist but is released from the body. The remedy for physical death is the resurrection, when the body will rejoin the soul.

The second type of death is spiritual death. Spiritual death is the separation of man from a relationship with God. It is spiritual death that was the consequence of Adam's sin of eating the fruit of the tree of the knowledge of good and evil (Genesis 2:17). All humans are born in this state. The remedy for spiritual death is salvation:

And you were dead in the trespasses and sins in which you once walked, following the course of this world, following the prince of the power of the air, the spirit that is now at work in the sons of disobedience—among whom we all once lived in the passions of our flesh, carrying out the desires of the body and the mind, and were by nature children of wrath, like the rest of mankind (Ephesians 2:1–3).

The last type of death is eternal death, also called the "second death." Eternal death is the permanent separation of man from a relationship with God. This is the permanent result of spiritual death and the rejection of God's saving grace. There is no remedy for eternal death. There are no second chances for spiritual life after physical death. See the following passages from Revelation:

"'He who has an ear, let him hear what the Spirit says to the churches. The one who conquers will not be hurt by the second death.'" (Revelation 2:11).

Blessed and holy is the one who shares in the first resurrection! Over such the second death has no power, but they will be priests of God and of Christ, and they will reign with him for a thousand years (Revelation 20:6).

Then Death and Hades were thrown into the lake of fire. This is the second death, the lake of fire. And if anyone's name was not found written in the book of life, he was thrown into the lake of fire (Revelation 20:14–15).

"But as for the cowardly, the faithless, the detestable, as for murderers, the sexually immoral, sorcerers, idolaters, and all liars, their portion will be in the lake that burns with fire and sulfur, which is the second death" (Revelation 21:8).

Intermediate State

The intermediate state is the conscious existence of the personality of both the godly and ungodly between the time of physical death and the resurrection at the Great White Throne Judgment. Physical death involves no loss of our immaterial consciousness (Revelation 6:9-11), and the soul of the redeemed passes immediately into the presence of Christ (Luke 23:43; Philippians 1:23; 2 Corinthians 5:8). There is a separation of soul and body (Philippians 1:21-24), and, for the redeemed, such separation will continue until the rapture (1 Thessalonians 4:13-17), which initiates the first resurrection (Revelation 20:4-6), when the soul and body of the believer will be reunited to be glorified forever with the Lord (Philippians 3:21; 1 Corinthians 15:35-44, 50-54). Until that time, the souls of the redeemed in Christ remain in joyful fellowship with our Lord Jesus Christ (2 Corinthians 5:8).

There are many who want to argue that, once we die, we are completely unconscious and without memory of our life. The thought is that we will not know we are dead because we will not exist anymore. Some like to argue the idea that, since we did not exist before we were born and had no consciousness, our death will be the same way. Some call this "soul sleep." However, John makes it clear, in the book of Revelation, that those who would be martyred for their faith will not only be conscious, but they will be aware of the life they lived on earth:

When he opened the fifth seal, I saw under the altar the souls of those who had been slain for the word of God and for the witness they had borne. They cried out with a loud voice, "O Sovereign Lord, holy and true, how long before you will judge and avenge our blood on those who dwell on the earth?" Then they were each given a white robe and told to rest a little longer, until the number of their fellow servants and their brothers should be complete, who were to be killed as they themselves had been (Revelation 6:9–11).

Following from the idea of "soul sleep," many like to claim that, when a person dies, he or she does not immediately enter into a temporary place awaiting final judgment. Once again, Scripture clearly speaks against this teaching. The Bible tells us that, the moment we die, we are either in the presence of the Lord or a temporary place of judgment.

This temporary place of judgement cannot be what is often taught to be a place called "purgatory," for the Bible tells us that there is no way out of this hell until the final judgment in the Lake of Fire. One cannot be prayed into or prayed out of this temporary judgment place. Through Christ's own words on the cross, we see that the thief crucified next to Him would be in Paradise with Christ that very day: *And he said to him, "Truly, I say to you, today you will be with me in paradise"* (Luke 23:43). We can also see that Paul expected himself and other believers to be with Christ immediately after death:

I am hard pressed between the two. My desire is to depart and be with Christ, for that is far better (Philippians 1:23).

Yes, we are of good courage, and we would rather be away from the body and at home with the Lord (2 Corinthians 5:8).

Lastly, to address the false claim that our bodies die and are not reunited with our spirits, God's Word makes it clear that our bodies will be transformed. People seem to think that once the physical body rots and decays that somehow the God who created everything from nothing cannot recreate our bodies. The God who created us from dirt the first time can recreate us from the dirt we become:

But our citizenship is in heaven, and from it we await a Savior, the Lord Jesus Christ, who will transform our lowly body to be like his glorious body, by the power that enables him even to subject all things to himself (Philippians 3:20-21).

But someone will ask, "How are the dead raised? With what kind of body do they come?" You foolish person! What you sow does not come to life unless it dies. And what you sow is not the body that is to be, but a bare kernel, perhaps of wheat or of some other grain. But God gives it a body as he has chosen, and to each kind of seed its own body. For not all flesh is the same, but there is one kind for humans, another for animals, another for birds, and another for fish. There are heavenly bodies and earthly bodies, but the glory of the heavenly is of one kind, and the glory of the earthly is of another. There is one glory of the sun, and another glory of the moon, and another glory of the stars; for star differs from star in glory. So is it with the resurrection of the dead. What is sown is perishable; what is raised is imperishable. It is sown in dishonor; it is raised in glory. It is sown in weakness; it is raised in power. It is sown a natural body; it is raised a spiritual body. If there is a natural body, there is also a spiritual body (1 Corinthians 15:35–44).

I tell you this, brothers: flesh and blood cannot inherit the kingdom of God, nor does the perishable inherit the imperishable. Behold! I tell you a mystery. We shall not all sleep, but we shall all be changed, in a moment, in the twinkling of an eye, at the last trumpet. For the trumpet will sound, and the dead will be raised imperishable, and we shall be changed. For this perishable body must put on the imperishable, and this mortal body must put on immortality. When the perishable puts on the imperishable, and the mortal puts on immortality, then shall come to pass the saying that is written: "Death is swallowed up in victory" (1 Corinthians 15:50–54).

Heaven

The righteous, at death, immediately enter into the presence of God. As we have seen, Christ told the thief on the cross next to Him that he would be in Paradise that very day when he died (Luke 23:43). Heaven is a temporary place of rest for the saints until the final rest in the eternal state (Revelation 14:13). See the following passages:

[...] and the dust returns to the earth as it was, and the spirit returns to God who gave it. (Ecclesiastes 12:7)

For we know that if the tent that is our earthly home is destroyed, we have a building from God, a house not made with hands, eternal in the heavens. For in this tent we groan, longing to put on our heavenly dwelling, if indeed by putting it on we may not be found naked. For while we are still in this tent, we groan, being burdened—not that we would be unclothed, but that we would be further clothed, so that what is mortal may be swallowed up by life. He who has prepared us for this very thing is God, who has given us the Spirit as a guarantee. So we are always of good courage. We know that while we are at home in the body we are away from the Lord, for we walk by faith, not by sight. Yes, we are of good courage, and we would rather be away from the body and at home with the Lord (2 Corinthians 5:1–8).

Hell

The wicked (unbelievers) at physical death immediately enter into hell, which is a place of restriction (1 Peter 3:19). Hell is a literal place where the soul consciously endures continuous torment as a consequence of sin. See the account of Lazarus and following verses:

"There was a rich man who was clothed in purple and fine linen and who feasted sumptuously every day. And at his gate was laid a poor man named

Lazarus, covered with sores, who desired to be fed with what fell from the rich man's table. Moreover, even the dogs came and licked his sores. The poor man died and was carried by the angels to Abraham's side. The rich man also died and was buried, and in Hades, being in torment, he lifted up his eyes and saw Abraham far off and Lazarus at his side. And he called out, 'Father Abraham, have mercy on me, and send Lazarus to dip the end of his finger in water and cool my tongue, for I am in anguish in this flame.' But Abraham said, 'Child, remember that you in your lifetime received your good things, and Lazarus in like manner bad things; but now he is comforted here, and you are in anguish. And besides all this, between us and you a great chasm has been fixed, in order that those who would pass from here to you may not be able, and none may cross from there to us.' And he said, 'Then I beg you, father, to send him to my father's house— for I have five brothers—so that he may warn them, lest they also come into this place of torment.' But Abraham said, 'They have Moses and the Prophets; let them hear them.' And he said, 'No, father Abraham, but if someone goes to them from the dead, they will repent.' He said to him, 'If they do not hear Moses and the Prophets, neither will they be convinced if someone should rise from the dead'" (Luke 16:19–31).

And if your hand causes you to sin, cut it off. It is better for you to enter life crippled than with two hands to go to hell, to the unquenchable fire (Mark 9:43).

And if your eye causes you to sin, tear it out. It is better for you to enter the kingdom of God with one eye than with two eyes to be thrown into hell, 'where their worm does not die and the fire is not quenched (Mark 9:47-48).

[...] then the Lord knows how to rescue the godly from trials, and to keep the unrighteous under punishment until the day of judgment (2 Peter 2:9).

Hell is different than the Lake of Fire. Hell is a temporary place of punishment, whereas the Lake of Fire is the eternal place of punishment. There is no path from Hell to Heaven. As Scripture tells us, there are different degrees of punishment in hell based upon the amount of knowledge each person had of God's Word while they were on earth:

"But I tell you that it will be more tolerable on the day of judgment for the land of Sodom than for you" (Matthew 11:24).

And that servant who knew his master's will but did not get ready or act according to his will, will receive a severe beating. But the one who did not know, and did what deserved a beating, will receive a light beating. Everyone to whom much was given, of him much will be required, and from him to whom they entrusted much, they will demand the more (Luke 12:47–48).

For all who have sinned without the law will also perish without the law, and all who have sinned under the law will be judged by the law (Romans 2:12).

Eternal state

The eternal state is ushered in by the Great White Throne Judgment. This judgment is the final judgment and the last event recorded in Scripture. At this Great White Throne Judgment the final and eternal place for the righteous and the unrighteous will be secured for all of eternity:

Then I saw a great white throne and him who was seated on it. From his presence earth and sky fled away, and no place was found for them. And I saw the dead, great and small, standing before the throne, and books were opened. Then another book was opened, which is the book of life. And the dead were judged by what was written in the books, according to what they had done. And the sea gave up the dead who were in it, Death and Hades gave up the dead who were in them, and they were judged, each one of them, according to what they had done. Then Death and Hades were thrown into the lake of fire. This is the second death, the lake of fire. And if anyone's name was not found written in the book of life, he was thrown into the lake of fire (Revelation 20:11–15).

There will be a bodily resurrection of all men—the saved to eternal life and the unsaved to judgment and everlasting punishment:

> *And this is the will of him who sent me, that I should lose nothing of all that he has given me, but raise it up on the last day* (John 6:39).

> *But if Christ is in you, although the body is dead because of sin, the Spirit is life because of righteousness. If the Spirit of him who raised Jesus from the dead dwells in you, he who raised Christ Jesus from the dead will also give life to your mortal bodies through his Spirit who dwells in you* (Romans 8:10–11).

> *For the creation waits with eager longing for the revealing of the sons of God. For the creation was subjected to futility, not willingly, but because of him who subjected it, in hope that the creation itself will be set free from its bondage to corruption and obtain the freedom of the glory of the children of God. For we know that the whole creation has been groaning together in the pains of childbirth until now. And not only the creation, but we ourselves, who have the firstfruits of the Spirit, groan inwardly as we wait eagerly for adoption as sons, the redemption of our bodies* (Romans 8:19–23).

> *[...] knowing that he who raised the Lord Jesus will raise us also with Jesus and bring us with you into his presence* (2 Corinthians 4:14).

And many of those who sleep in the dust of the earth shall awake, some to everlasting life, and some to shame and everlasting contempt (Daniel 12:2).

[...] and come out, those who have done good to the resurrection of life, and those who have done evil to the resurrection of judgment (John 5:29).

At death, the souls of the unsaved are kept under punishment until the second resurrection (Luke 16:19-26; Revelation 20:13-15), when the soul and the resurrection body will be united (John 5:28-29). They shall then appear at the Great White Throne Judgment (Revelation 20:11-15) and shall be cast into the Lake of Fire (Matthew 25:41-46), cut off from the life of God forever (Daniel 12:2; Matthew 25:41-46; 2 Thessalonians 1:7-9).

The Lake of Fire

There is a literal place known as the Lake of Fire, where both men and angels will be consciously punished—in both body (for men) and spirit—for their sin in a real, everlasting, tormenting lake of fire. It is important to note that Hell is a temporary place of punishment until the Great White Throne Judgment. Then, the inhabitants of Hell will be cast into the Lake of Fire for all eternity:

Then I saw a great white throne and him who was seated on it. From his presence earth and sky fled away, and no place was found for them. And I saw the dead, great and small, standing before the throne, and books were opened. Then another book was opened, which is the book of life. And the dead were judged by what was written in the books, according to what they had done. And the sea gave up the dead who were in it, Death and Hades gave up the dead who were in them, and they were judged, each one of them, according to what they had done. Then Death and Hades were thrown into the lake of fire. This is the second death, the lake of fire. And if anyone's name was not found written in the book of life, he was thrown into the lake of fire (Revelation 20:11–15).

"But as for the cowardly, the faithless, the detestable, as for murderers, the sexually immoral, sorcerers, idolaters, and all liars, their portion will be in the lake that burns with fire and sulfur, which is the second death" (Revelation 21:8).

Judgment is based on works. So, many people wrongly think that God will see their works as good and merit them eternal life because of these good works. They don't realize, however, that the works in which they trust will be the very things that condemn them: *"the dead were judged according to their works, by the things which were written in the books"* (Revelation 20:12).

The problem with trusting in works is that no works are good enough to merit salvation:

From of old no one has heard or perceived by the ear, no eye has seen a God besides you, who acts for those who wait for him (Isaiah 64:4).

For by grace you have been saved through faith. And this is not your own doing; it is the gift of God, not a result of works, so that no one may boast (Ephesians 2:8–9).

[...] he saved us, not because of works done by us in righteousness, but according to his own mercy, by the washing of regeneration and renewal of the Holy Spirit (Titus 3:5).

New Heavens, New Earth, and New Jerusalem

There is also a literal place known as the New Heavens, the New Earth, and the New Jerusalem where persons, both men and angels, will consciously worship God in His real and everlasting presence. This will be a place where God is the center of all worship and purpose for being. People will enjoy worshiping God, but it will not be a place about man or his enjoyment; it will be about God:

"For behold, I create new heavens and a new earth, and the former things shall not be remembered or come into mind" (Isaiah 65:17).

"For as the new heavens and the new earth that I make shall remain before me, says the Lord, so shall your offspring and your name remain" (Isaiah 66:22).

But according to his promise we are waiting for new heavens and a new earth in which righteousness dwells (2 Peter 3:13).

The one who conquers, I will make him a pillar in the temple of my God. Never shall he go out of it, and I will write on him the name of my God, and the name of the city of my God, the new Jerusalem, which comes down from my God out of heaven, and my own new name (Revelation 3:12).

Then I saw a new heaven and a new earth, for the first heaven and the first earth had passed away, and the sea was no more. And I saw the holy city, new Jerusalem, coming down out of heaven from God, prepared as a bride adorned for her husband (Revelation 21:1–2).

Scripture tells us that, in this place, there will be no marriage. Therefore, there will be a change in our human relationships; we will not continue in the same relationship structure that we had on earth. Although we will see and recognize family members, the relationship will be changed because the focus will be on God, not on man:

For in the resurrection they neither marry nor are given in marriage, but are like angels in heaven (Matthew 22:30).

For when they rise from the dead, they neither marry nor are given in marriage, but are like angels in heaven (Mark 12:25).

Judgment is based on having your name in the Lamb's Book of Life. A person having their name in this book grants the person entrance into this eternal resting place, sometimes called the "everlasting rest." As discussed in chapter 6 on the subject of salvation, having your name written in the Book of Life is granted to those in Christ. See the following references:

The one who conquers will be clothed thus in white garments, and I will never blot his name out of the book of life. I will confess his name before my Father and before his angels (Revelation 3:5).

[...] and all who dwell on earth will worship it, everyone whose name has not been written before the foundation of the world in the book of life of the Lamb who was slain (Revelation 13:8).

The beast that you saw was, and is not, and is about to rise from the bottomless pit and go to destruction. And the dwellers on earth whose names have not been written in the book of life from the foundation of the world will marvel to see the beast, because it was and is not and is to come (Revelation 17:8).

But nothing unclean will ever enter it, nor anyone who does what is detestable or false, but only those who are written in the Lamb's book of life (Revelation 21:27).

[...] and if anyone takes away from the words of the book of this prophecy, God will take away his share in the tree of life and in the holy city, which are described in this book (Revelation 22:19).

From beginning to end, we see that God not only created the universe but has a plan for all time. We are not purposeless beings, but instead, we are people created in the image of God in order that we may have eternal life.

Endnotes

[1] House, H. Wayne, <u>Charts of Cults, Sects & Religious Movements;</u> Zondervan Publishing House, Grand Rapids, Michigan; p. 301.

[2]   http://danielbwallace.com/2013/09/09/the-number-of-textual-variants-an-evangelical-miscalculation

[3]   http://danielbwallace.com/2013/09/09/the-number-of-textual-variants-an-evangelical-miscalculation

[4] Aslan, Reza, "Zealot: The Life and Times of Jesus of Nazareth" (Random House, 2013), XXVII.

[5] https://carm.org/bible-text-manuscript-tree

[6] Wallace, D. B. (2011). Lost in Transmission: How Badly Did the Scribes Corrupt the New Testament Text? In D. B. Wallace (Ed.), *Revisiting the Corruption of the New Testament: Manuscript, Patristic, and Apocryphal Evidence* (p. 28). Grand Rapids, MI: Kregel Academic & Professional.

[7] Pfeiffer, Charles F. *Wycliffe Bible Encyclopedia*. Chicago, IL: Moody Press, 1975.

[8] Unger, Merrill F. *The New Unger's Bible Dictionary*. Chicago, IL: The Moody Bible Institute of Chicago, 1998, c1988.

[9] Josephus, F., & Whiston, W. (1996, c1987). *The works of Josephus: Complete and unabridged*. Includes index. (Ant 18.63-64). Peabody: Hendrickson.

[10] Arndt, W., Danker, F. W., & Bauer, W. (2000). A Greek-English lexicon of the New Testament and other early Christian literature. Chicago: University of Chicago Press.

[11] Zodhiates, S. (2000). The complete word study dictionary: New Testament. Chattanooga, TN: AMG Publishers.

[12] Moulton, J. H., & Milligan, G. (1930). The vocabulary of the Greek Testament. London: Hodder and Stoughton.

[13] Bromiley, G. W. (Ed.). (1979–1988). In The International Standard Bible Encyclopedia, Revised. Wm. B. Eerdmans.

[14] Bromiley, ibid.

[15] John Calvin, Institutes of the Christian Religion (1559), Translated by Henry Beveridge, Wm. B. Eerdmans, Grand Rapids, Michigan, Page 289

[16] Grudem, W. A. (2004). *Systematic theology: an introduction to biblical doctrine* (pp. 865–866). Leicester, England; Grand Rapids, MI: Inter-Varsity Press; Zondervan Pub. House.

Made in the USA
Columbia, SC
14 February 2024

31835568R00107